# RICARDO
*Meals for Every Occasion*

whitecap

English edition published in Canada in 2009 by Whitecap Books
First published in French in 2008 by Les Éditions La Presse

**Library and Archives Canada Cataloguing in Publication**

Ricardo, 1967-
    Ricardo : meals for every occasion / Ricardo
Larrivée ; Matt Sendbuehler, translator.

Translation of: Ricardo, cuisiner en toutes circonstances.
Includes index.
ISBN 978-1-55285-964-3

    1. Cookery.   I. Title.

TX714.R53 2009          641.5          C2009-900483-6


The publisher acknowledges the financial support of the Government of Canada through
the Book Publishing Industry Development Program (BPIDP) and the Province of British Columbia
through the Book Publishing Tax Credit.

Printed in Canada

09 10 11 12 13    5 4 3 2 1

CHRISTIAN LACROIX
*photography*

SONIA BLUTEAU
*art direction*

BRIGITTE COUTU
*editor*

**AUTHOR**
Ricardo Larrivée

**PUBLISHER**
Martin Balthazar

**ART DIRECTORS AND DESIGNERS**
Sonia Bluteau, Caroline Nault

**PHOTOGRAPHER**
Christian Lacroix
lisemadore.com

**FOOD STYLIST**
Anne Gagné

**ACCESSORIES STYLIST**
Sylvain Riel

**GRAPHIC DESIGNERS**
Caroline Blanchette, Ginette Cabana

**ASSISTANT FOOD STYLIST**
Étienne Marquis

**ASSISTANT PHOTOGRAPHER**
François-Nicolas Dionne

**ILLUSTRATOR**
Caroline Nault

**KITCHEN TEAM**
Kareen Grondin, Étienne Marquis, Nataly Simard, Antoine Côté-Robitaille

**TRANSLATION AND EDITING**
Matt Sendbuehler, Andrew Mullins, Karen Loeb, Craig Schweickert

**PROOFREADER**
Naomi Pauls

Our sincere thanks for their invaluable assistance:
Ares, Arthur Quentin, L'Atelier du Presbytère, The Bay, Canadian Tire, Comme la vie avec un accent, Déco Découverte, Després Laporte, Farfelu, HomeSense, IKEA, La Maison d'Émilie, Métro Collin, Moutarde Décor, Pier 1, Pierre Belvédère, Quincaillerie Dante, Stacaro, Les Touilleurs, Trois Fois Passera, Vinum Design, Z'axe, Zone.

# ding dong

We all know the feeling of dread brought on by the sound of the doorbell +++ Aunt Nancy just decided to drop by, right around 5 o'clock +++ Your buddy Peter always shows up late, his latest flame in tow—and she happens to be vegetarian, or afflicted with a rare food allergy +++ Or there's your dear mother-in-law, who's only happy with her own cooking +++ This book is dedicated to everyone who loves to have company, but also to those who are afraid of having guests and have sworn that they've entertained for the last time. Because there's always a next time. After all, having people over to share a meal is one of life's great pleasures, and we all have to play host sooner or later. +++ RICARDO

CON
TEN
TS

Having people over for dinner is tough. You dirty tons of dishes—mostly the nice, fragile stuff that doesn't go in the dishwasher. You get stains on your best white tablecloth. You discover a pile of potato chip crumbs under the sofa cushions. But, then again, the whole thing takes place within the confines of the living room-kitchen-dining room triangle. It's a manageable space, where you can usually keep potential mishaps in your line of sight. But when the unexpected happens—a blizzard, relatives come from far away, the 13th bottle of wine gets popped—and you're suddenly having overnight guests, things can get really hairy. A house that was already a war zone is now a nursery full of adults who are practically as helpless as babes in arms. You're digging out a towel for one, finding a pillow for another, turning up the thermostat for Auntie (never mind that the rest of us are suffocating) and showing your cousin how to work the remote. Exhausted, you're the last to tumble into bed. And that's just the start. Because guess who's making breakfast? Nope, there's no way they'll feed themselves; they're all too shy to even peek inside the fridge. Fortunately, there's a flip side to every situation: this could actually be fun. After all, we love 'em to pieces.

OH, NO! They're sleeping OVER!

# breakfast and brunch recipes

# ORANGE AND GRAPEFRUIT SALAD WITH A TWIST

*Preparation* 30 MINUTES          *Serves* 6

1/4 honeydew melon, peeled
2 pink grapefruit
2 white grapefruit
4 oranges
Grated zest of 1/2 lime
1 Tbsp (15 mL) sugar (optional)
Mint leaves to garnish

**1** Using a vegetable peeler, cut the melon into shavings. Cut these in half as needed. Set aside.
**2** Peel the grapefruit and oranges to bare the flesh. To do this, slice off both ends of the fruit. Stand the fruit on a board. Cut the peel as close to the flesh as possible, removing the white membrane completely. Slide the blade of a knife between each of the section membranes and lift out each section. Work over a bowl to collect all the juice.
**3** Add the citrus fruit to the bowl. Add the melon, lime zest and sugar (if using). Toss gently. Refrigerate until ready to serve.
**4** Garnish with mint leaves.

# CRANBERRY SCONES

*Preparation* 20 MINUTES     *Cooking* 15 TO 20 MINUTES     *Makes* 20 SCONES

## Scones

2-1/2 cups (625 mL) unbleached all-purpose flour
1/2 cup (125 mL) sugar
2 tsp (10 mL) baking powder
1/2 tsp (2.5 mL) salt
1/2 cup (125 mL) cold unsalted butter, cubed
3/4 cup (180 mL) buttermilk
1/2 cup (125 mL) dried cranberries

## Glaze

2 Tbsp (30 mL) buttermilk
1 Tbsp (15 mL) sugar

**1** With the rack in the middle position, preheat the oven to 400°F (200°C). Line a cookie sheet with parchment paper.

**2 SCONES** In a food processor, combine the flour, sugar, baking powder and salt. Add the butter and pulse until the butter pieces are pea-sized. Add the buttermilk and pulse just long enough to moisten the flour. Transfer to a bowl and fold in the cranberries. Do not overmix.

**3** On a floured surface, flatten the dough with your hands or roll out to about 3/4 inch (2 cm) thick. Using a 2-inch (5 cm) round cookie cutter, cut the dough into rounds. Arrange the rounds on the baking sheet, leaving space between each one.

**4 GLAZE** Brush with buttermilk and sprinkle with sugar. Bake until golden brown, 15 to 20 minutes. Let cool on a rack.

**5** Serve with Honey–Orange Butter (page 023). You can freeze the scones.

# HONEY-ORANGE BUTTER

*Preparation* 5 MINUTES      *Refrigeration* 10 MINUTES      *Makes* 2/3 CUP (150 ML)

1/2 cup (125 mL) butter, softened
2 Tbsp (30 mL) honey
1 Tbsp (15 mL) orange juice
Grated zest of 1 orange

**1** In a bowl or a small food processor, mix all ingredients until thoroughly combined. Transfer to a ramekin and refrigerate for about 10 minutes.
**2** Serve with toast, croissants or Cranberry Scones (page 021).

RECIPE P027

# MANGO AND STRAWBERRY SMOOTHIES

*Preparation* 10 MINUTES

**On those days when you don't feel like making breakfast, you can make individual portions of these smoothies (they're easy and nutritious). Here are the recipes for one or six servings.**

*Serves* 1

*Mango smoothie*
1/2 cup (125 mL) frozen mango
2 Tbsp (30 mL) soft tofu
1/3 cup (75 mL) milk
2 tsp (10 mL) sugar or honey

*Strawberry smoothie*
1/2 cup (125 mL) frozen strawberries
2 Tbsp (30 mL) soft tofu
1/4 cup (60 mL) milk
2 tsp (10 mL) sugar or honey

*Serves* 6

3 cups (750 mL)
3/4 cup (180 mL)
2 cups (500 mL)
1/4 cup (60 mL)

3 cups (750 mL)
3/4 cup (180 mL)
1-1/2 cups (375 mL)
1/4 cup (60 mL)

**1 MANGO SMOOTHIE** Purée all the ingredients in a blender. Depending on the quantity you are making, pour the smoothie into 1 or 6 large glasses (about 1-1/4 cups/310 mL each).
**2 STRAWBERRY SMOOTHIE** Purée all the ingredients in a blender.
**3** Slowly pour the strawberry smoothie over the back of a spoon into the glass or glasses.
**4** Drink through straws.

# QUICK STRAWBERRY-MAPLE SYRUP JAM

*Preparation* 10 MINUTES          *Cooking* 18 MINUTES          *Makes* ABOUT 2 CUPS (500 ML)

**Homemade jam for the lazy gourmet. Just throw three parts berries in a saucepan (strawberries, raspberries, blueberries) along with one part maple syrup. Simmer for 15 minutes. That's it. Life is good. Thank you, Marie-Soleil, for serving me this jam one sunny summer morning at the cottage.**

3 cups (750 mL) hulled and quartered fresh strawberries or frozen strawberries (or raspberries, blueberries or other berries)
1 cup (250 mL) maple syrup

**1** In a saucepan, bring the berries and syrup to a boil. Simmer over medium heat until the mixture thickens slightly, about 15 minutes. Let cool.

# BUCKWHEAT CRÊPE BURRITOS

*Preparation* 30 MINUTES    *Cooking* 30 MINUTES    *Serves* 8 TO 10

*Buckwheat crêpes*
6 cups (1.5 L) milk
3 eggs
3 cups (750 mL) buckwheat flour
2 tsp (10 mL) baking powder
Salt

*Filling*
2 onions, chopped
1 lb (500 g) brown mushrooms, sliced
8 slices bacon, coarsely chopped
1/4 cup (60 mL) olive oil
1 Tbsp (15 mL) finely chopped fresh chives
1-1/2 lb (675 g) sausage meat (Toulouse, Italian, breakfast, etc.)
2 cups (500 mL) grated sharp cheddar
1-1/2 cups (375 mL) applesauce
Molasses

**1 BUCKWHEAT CRÊPES**  Preheat the oven to 200°F (100°C) for keeping the crêpes and filling warm.

**2** In a bowl, whisk together all ingredients until the batter is smooth. While cooking the crêpes, stir the batter from time to time to prevent the flour from settling.

**3** Ladle about 1/4 cup (60 mL) of batter into a well-buttered, preheated 9-inch (23 cm) non-stick skillet. Cook the crêpe on both sides. Repeat with the remaining batter, stacking each crêpe on a serving plate as you go. Keep the plate in the oven, covered with foil.

**4 FILLING**  In a large non-stick skillet, brown the onions, mushrooms and bacon in 2 Tbsp (30 mL) oil. Add the chives. Season with salt and pepper. Transfer to a serving bowl. Cover and set aside in the warm oven.

**5** In the same skillet, brown the sausage meat in 2 Tbsp (30 mL) oil, breaking it up with a fork. Transfer to a serving bowl and keep warm.

**6** Place the cheddar, applesauce and molasses in separate bowls.

**7** Place the crêpes and fillings in the centre of the table. Diners garnish their own crêpes.

# SUNDAE BRUNCH

*Preparation* 20 MINUTES     *Serves* 4

1-1/2 cups (375 mL) fresh raspberries
3 Tbsp (45 mL) sugar
1 Tbsp (15 mL) lemon juice
1/2 cup (125 mL) Granola (recipe follows)
2 cups (500 mL) vanilla frozen yogurt

**1** Place 4 sundae glasses in the freezer for 10 minutes.
**2** Meanwhile, in a bowl, gently toss the raspberries, sugar and lemon juice. Let stand for 10 minutes.
**3** Place a scoop of frozen yogurt in each sundae glass. Sprinkle with three-quarters of the granola and berries. Add a second scoop of frozen yogurt. Top with the remaining granola and berries. Serve as a brunch dessert. Kids will love it.

# GRANOLA

*Preparation* 15 MINUTES     *Cooking* 35 TO 40 MINUTES     *Makes* ABOUT 6 CUPS (1.5 L)

3 cups (750 mL) rolled oats
1 cup (250 mL) slivered almonds
1/2 cup (125 mL) unsalted pistachios
1/2 cup (125 mL) sunflower seeds
1/2 cup (125 mL) maple syrup
1/4 cup (60 mL) unsalted butter, melted
1/2 cup (125 mL) raisins
1/2 cup (125 mL) dried cranberries

**1** With the rack in the middle position, preheat the oven to 325°F (170°C). Line a cookie sheet with parchment paper.
**2** In a bowl, combine the oats, almonds, pistachios and sunflower seeds. Add the syrup and butter and stir to combine. Spread the mixture on the cookie sheet. Bake for 35 to 40 minutes, stirring every 10 minutes, until golden brown. Let cool completely. Add the dried fruit.
**3** Serve as a breakfast cereal or as a topping for Sundae Brunch (above).

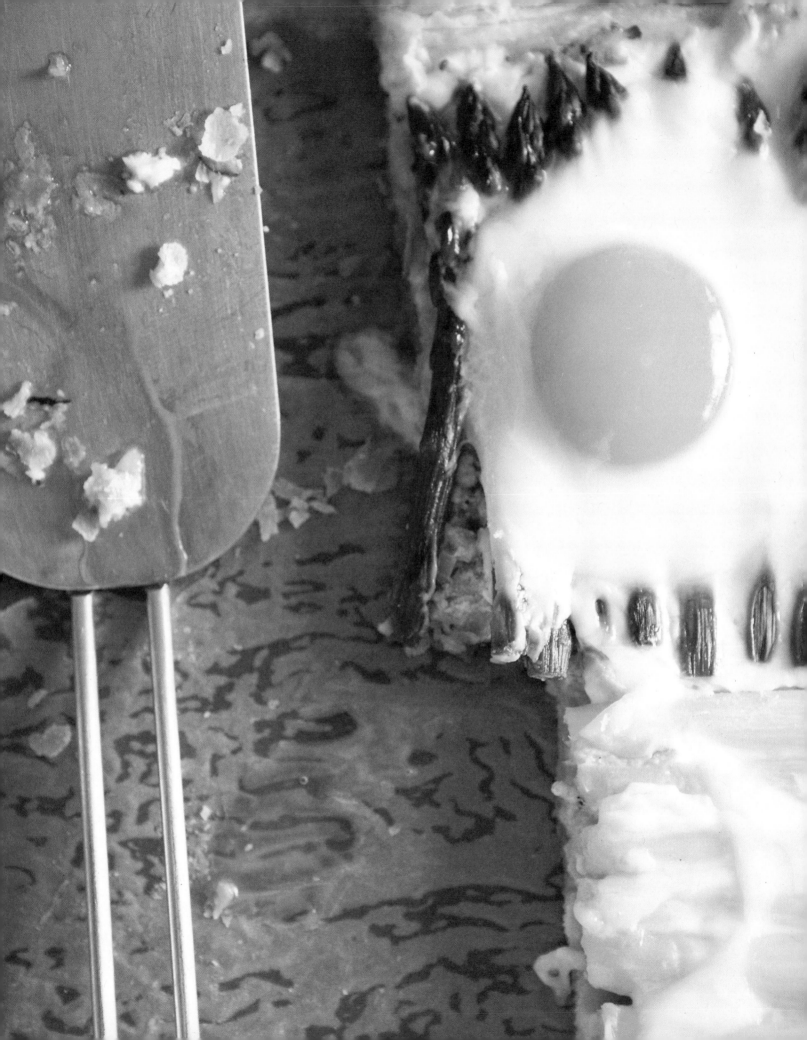

# QUILT PIE WITH ASPARAGUS, EGGS AND HAM

*Preparation* 25 MINUTES          *Refrigeration* 30 MINUTES          *Cooking* 45 MINUTES          *Serves* 6

**I'm always on the lookout for practical ways to cook eggs for a large group. Not only is this dish a great way to do just that, it happens to be spectacular.**

14 oz (400 g) store-bought puff pastry dough, thawed
2 onions, thinly sliced
2 Tbsp (30 mL) olive oil
1/2 lb (225 g) sliced Black Forest ham, chopped
1/2 cup (125 mL) sour cream
1/4 cup (60 mL) whole-grain mustard
24 to 36 small green asparagus spears, each 5 inches (12 cm) long, trimmed
24 to 36 small white asparagus spears, each 5 inches (12 cm) long, trimmed
6 eggs
Salt and pepper

**1** Line a 12- x 17-inch (30 x 43 cm) baking sheet with parchment paper.
**2** On a floured surface, roll the dough into a 12- x 17-inch (30 x 43 cm) rectangle. Place it on the baking sheet. Fold the edges of the dough inward, making a 1/2-inch (1 cm) upturned edge. Refrigerate for 30 minutes.
**3** In a skillet over medium heat, brown the onions in the oil. Season with salt and pepper. Let cool.
**4** In a bowl, combine the onions, ham, sour cream and mustard. Refrigerate.
**5** In a pot of boiling salted water, blanch the asparagus for 1 to 2 minutes. Transfer the spears to a bowl of ice water. Drain and set aside.
**6** With the rack in the middle position, preheat the oven to 400°F (200°C).
**7** Spread the ham mixture evenly over the dough. Place the baking sheet next to the work surface, with a long side parallel to the edge of the counter or table.
**8 ASSEMBLY** Mentally divide the pie into six 5-inch (12 cm) squares. Working from left to right, lay about 8 green asparagus spears side by side in the first square. In the next square, lay 8 white asparagus spears side by side, at a right angle to the green asparagus. Repeat with the remaining squares, alternating colours and directions to create a quilt effect.
**9** Bake for 25 minutes. Remove from the oven. Crack an egg onto each square. Bake for about 10 more minutes. Cut into 6 squares and serve.

RECIPE P039

# BREAKFAST CLUB SANDWICHES

*Preparation* 15 MINUTES     *Cooking* 20 MINUTES     *Serves* 6

**There's no mess quite like the one you make frying bacon in a skillet. To avoid splattering grease all over the kitchen, my trick is to place strips of bacon on a cookie sheet and bake them. They don't need as much attention and will stay nice and straight. Plus, you'll look like a food-styling genius.**

18 slices bacon (about one 1 lb/454 g package)
12 eggs, lightly beaten
3/4 cup (180 mL) mayonnaise
Salt and pepper
18 slices square white bread
18 slices tomato
12 leaves Boston lettuce
Toothpicks

**1** With the rack in the middle position, preheat the oven to 425°F (220°C). Line a rimmed baking sheet with parchment paper. Line a 10- x 15-inch (25 x 38 cm) casserole dish with parchment paper, leaving paper hanging over 2 sides. Oil the paper and sides of the dish.
**2** Lay the slices of bacon on the baking sheet. Bake until golden and crisp, 12 to 14 minutes. Drain on paper towels. Set aside.
**3** In a bowl, mix the eggs and 1/4 cup (60 mL) of the mayonnaise. Season with salt and pepper.
**4** Pour the egg mixture into the baking dish and bake until set but still moist, 10 to 12 minutes. Cut the omelette into 6 portions. Set aside. Turn off the oven and return the bacon to the oven to reheat it.
**5 ASSEMBLY** Toast 3 slices of bread and spread with mayonnaise. Top 1 slice of bread with the egg and 3 slices of bacon. Cover with a second slice of bread. Top with 3 tomato slices and 2 lettuce leaves. Top with a third slice of bread. Insert toothpicks into the centre of the 4 corners of the sandwich and cut the sandwich into triangles. Repeat with the remaining ingredients.

# FIDDLEHEAD OMELETTE

*Preparation* 15 MINUTES  *Cooking* 20 MINUTES  *Serves* 4

You can make this "omelette of the day" with any vegetable you want. Just sauté it beforehand in a little butter or olive oil. Add some cheese, and you'll be thanking me. Since you're not in a restaurant kitchen or a three-ring circus, forget the star-chef acrobatics—don't try to make a gigantic omelette and flip it. Instead, get two skillets going and make two at once. They're much easier to cook and divvy up.

**Filling**
1/2 lb (225 g) fiddleheads
1/2 lb (225 g) bacon, cut in 1/2-inch (1 cm) pieces
1 small onion, finely sliced
1 Tbsp (15 mL) finely chopped fresh chives
Salt and pepper

**Omelette**
12 eggs, lightly beaten
1/4 cup (60 mL) half-and-half cream (10%) or milk
1 Tbsp (15 mL) finely chopped flat-leaf parsley
2 Tbsp (30 mL) butter
1-1/2 cups (375 mL) grated Gruyère cheese (optional)
Salt and pepper

**1 FILLING** Blanch the fiddleheads in boiling salted water for about 2 minutes. Drain and rinse under cold running water. Set aside.
**2** Brown the bacon in a skillet over medium heat. Pour off the rendered fat. Add the onion and sauté until tender. Add the fiddleheads and chives. Sauté for 1 or 2 minutes. Season with salt and pepper. Set aside.
**3 OMELETTE** In a bowl, whisk together the eggs, cream and parsley. Season with salt and pepper.
**4** Melt the butter in 2 preheated 12-inch (30 cm) non-stick skillets. Pour half the eggs into each skillet. Cook over medium heat for 1 to 2 minutes, using a spatula to pull apart the omelettes and let the uncooked egg run to the bottom. When the edges (not the centre) of the omelettes are almost done, sprinkle 1 side of each with half of the filling and half of the Gruyère. Using the spatula, fold the omelettes over the filling and slide onto plates.

# PEANUT BUTTER AND BANANA MUFFINS WITH STRAWBERRY JAM

***Preparation*** 20 MINUTES      ***Cooking*** 30 MINUTES      ***Makes*** 12 MUFFINS

1 very ripe banana
2 tsp (10 mL) lemon juice
1-1/2 cups (375 mL) unbleached all-purpose flour
1-1/2 tsp (7.5 mL) baking powder
1/2 cup (125 mL) unsalted butter, softened
1 cup (250 mL) brown sugar
1/2 cup (125 mL) peanut butter
2 eggs
1/2 cup (125 mL) milk
1/2 tsp (2.5 mL) vanilla extract
1/3 cup (75 mL) chopped roasted peanuts
2 bananas, peeled and sliced
Homemade (page 027) or store-bought strawberry jam

**1** With the rack in the middle position, preheat the oven to 375°F (190°C). Line 12 muffin cups with paper liners.
**2** In a bowl, coarsely mash the banana with the lemon juice. Set aside.
**3** In another bowl, combine the flour and baking powder. Set aside.
**4** In a third bowl, cream the butter with the brown sugar and peanut butter using an electric mixer. Add the eggs 1 at a time, beating until the mixture is smooth.
**5** With the mixer on low speed, mix the dry ingredients, alternating with the mashed bananas, milk and vanilla.
**6** Divide the batter among the muffin cups. Sprinkle with peanuts. Bake until a toothpick inserted in the centre of a muffin comes out clean, about 30 minutes. Unmould and let cool on a rack.
**7** Serve with the banana slices and strawberry jam.

# CHEDDAR AND ONION BAGUETTES

*Preparation* 15 MINUTES    *Cooking* 15 MINUTES    *Serves* 4

*Caramelized onions*
2 onions, thinly sliced
3 Tbsp (45 mL) butter
1 Tbsp (15 mL) cider vinegar
Salt and pepper

*Honey–mustard spread*
2 Tbsp (30 mL) Dijon mustard
1 Tbsp (15 mL) whole-grain mustard
1 Tbsp (15 mL) honey
Pinch ground turmeric

*Sandwiches*
1 baguette
1/2 lb (225 g) sharp cheddar, sliced
8 slices bacon, fried until crisp
1 green onion, finely sliced
1 Tbsp (15 mL) olive oil

**1 CARAMELIZED ONIONS** In a skillet over low heat, brown the onions in the butter until caramelized, 10 to 15 minutes. Add the vinegar. Cook for about 2 more minutes. Season with salt and pepper. Set aside.
**2 HONEY–MUSTARD SPREAD** In a bowl, combine all the ingredients. Set aside.
**3 SANDWICHES** Using a bread knife, cut the baguette into 4 equal lengths. Slice each piece in half horizontally. Spread lightly with honey–mustard spread. Garnish with onions, cheddar, bacon and green onions. Close the sandwiches.
**4** In a large skillet over medium heat, brown the sandwiches on each side in the oil. Press with a spatula. Fry until the cheese melts.

We all have an insurance policy to protect us in case of fire, burglary, or a laundry hookup that wasn't tightened quite right. But nobody has insurance to cover a much more likely emergency: the friend who decides to stay for dinner. Spur-of-the-moment entertaining can be a high-stakes diplomatic juggling act that puts you at risk of losing everything: your pride, your friends, an evening and even your reputation. Friends drop by after work. You shoot the breeze, share some laughs. Time flies. It's almost 6 o'clock. Suddenly hunger takes over and you pipe up. The fateful words spill out all by themselves: "Would you like to stay for dinner?" Before you even have time to panic, you hear a delighted chorus of "Of course!" Then the gravity of the situation sinks in. You haven't got a thing to serve. Too late. Sure, you can talk about "keeping it casual," but everybody knows that's code for "three-day-old leftovers." Thank God, there are ways to save face. And I don't mean the delivery menu from the local pizza joint. What you need is an "emergency kit" in your pantry and, above all, an arsenal of last-minute recipes.

# quick and easy dinners

SPEND FIVE MINUTES EXAMINING THE INSIDE OF YOUR FRIDGE, AND YOU'LL LEARN MORE ABOUT YOURSELF THAN YOU WOULD AFTER FIVE YEARS OF THERAPY. THE CONTENTS OF THE FRIDGE, FREEZER AND PANTRY ARE LIKE A MIRROR OF THE PEOPLE IN THE HOUSE; THEY VARY WITH OUR EATING HABITS. THOSE WHO PRIDE THEMSELVES ON BEING READY FOR ANYTHING WILL HAVE SEVERAL MONTHS' WORTH OF SURVIVAL RATIONS. OTHERS HAVE CANS DEEP IN THE PANTRY WHOSE LABELS ARE JUST ABOUT READY FOR THE *ANTIQUES ROADSHOW.* AND THEN THERE ARE THOSE WHO HAVE ALL THEY NEED TO IMPROVISE A GREAT MEAL WITHOUT BREAKING A SWEAT. WHEN YOU'VE GOT LAST-MINUTE COMPANY, IT'S PERFECTLY OK TO DASH TO THE STORE AND PICK UP SOMETHING FRESH TO ROUND OUT WHAT YOU HAVE ON HAND. I MADE THE FOLLOWING LISTS WITH MY KIND OF COOKING AND THE RECIPES IN THIS BOOK IN MIND.

# pantry

TETRA PAKS OF CHICKEN BROTH (FOR SOUPS, SAUCES, RICE AND RISOTTO) CANNED TOMATOES (FOR A QUICK PASTA SAUCE OR SOUP) CANNED LEGUMES (FOR SALADS AND CLEAN-OUT-THE-FRIDGE SOUPS) PASTA AND RICE ASSORTED VINEGARS (BALSAMIC, WINE, RICE . . .) COCONUT MILK CHOCOLATE HONEY JARS OF MORELLO CHERRIES IN SYRUP (FOR CHERRY FLAMBÉES, SUNDAES, ETC.) GARLIC AND ONIONS

# refrigerator

HEAVY CREAM (35%) (WHIP IT TO DECORATE CAKES OR TOP OTHER DESSERTS) LEMONS AND LIMES ASIAN SAUCES (SOY, HOISIN, SAMBAL OELEK) A CHUNK OF FRESH PARMESAN (OR GRATED PARMESAN, KEPT IN THE FREEZER) EGGS THICK PLAIN YOGURT (FOR DIPS, SAUCES AND DESSERTS) INEXPENSIVE WHITE WINE (FOR DEGLAZING, RISOTTO, SAUCES) APPLES DIJON MUSTARD FRESH GINGER

# FREEZER

SKINLESS, BONELESS CHICKEN BREASTS PEELED, DEVEINED SHRIMP VACUUM-PACKED WHITEFISH FILLETS INDIVIDUALLY WRAPPED PORK TENDERLOINS INDIVIDUALLY FROZEN STRIPS OF BACON BERRIES (FOR SAUCES, MOUSSES, SMOOTHIES AND PIES) TOMATO SAUCE (FOR PASTA, PIZZA, ROSÉ SAUCE) FROZEN PEAS (RISOTTO, SIDE VEGETABLE) GRATED MOZZARELLA PHYLLO OR PUFF PASTRY DOUGH VANILLA ICE CREAM

# DUKKA

*Preparation* 10 MINUTES     *Serves* 6 TO 8

For years now, the trio of bread, olive oil and balsamic vinegar has been the standard nibble to keep hunger at bay during cocktails. But times are changing. Introducing *dukka*, a blend of spices and crushed almonds in which you dip a piece of bread dipped in olive oil. I first encountered it in New Zealand, where it shows up on every restaurant table. Make sure you always have the ingredients on hand. It may be last-minute, but it's super classy.

2/3 cup (150 mL) whole blanched almonds
2 Tbsp (30 mL) sesame seeds
4 tsp (20 mL) chili powder
2 tsp (10 mL) turmeric
1 tsp (5 mL) onion salt
1 tsp (5 mL) celery salt
1 tsp (5 mL) cumin
1 tsp (5 mL) ground coriander
Cayenne pepper to taste
Olive oil
Cubed bread for dipping

**1** Using a mortar and pestle or a small food processor, crush the almonds into small pieces. Add the remaining ingredients except the olive oil and bread, and mix well. Transfer to a small bowl. Pour the olive oil into another bowl. Serve with bread cubes that diners dip first in the oil and then in the *dukka*.

aromatic
BUT NOT
HOT

# RED BELL PEPPER SPREAD

*Preparation* 10 MINUTES   *Cooking* 15 MINUTES   *Makes* ABOUT 1-1/2 CUPS (375 ML)

**After I developed and tasted this spread, I told myself it was too simple to be a proper recipe—it only had two ingredients. So I tried adding all sorts of things, but I eventually wound up back at square one. Sometimes, simpler really is better.**

4 red bell peppers, halved and cored
1/4 cup (60 mL) olive oil
Salt and pepper

**1** With the rack in the top position, preheat the broiler. Line a baking sheet with parchment paper.
**2** Place the peppers on the baking sheet, skin side up. Brush lightly with oil. Broil until the skins blacken, about 15 minutes.
**3** Place the peppers in an airtight container. Let cool and slide the skins off.
**4** In a food processor, purée the peppers with the remaining oil. Season with salt and pepper. Serve with mini pitas, spread on slices of baguette as hors d'oeuvres or as a dip for crudités.

# FISH STRACCIATELLA WITH HERBS

*Preparation* 15 MINUTES     *Cooking* 10 MINUTES     *Serves* 4

5 cups (1.25 L) chicken broth
6 leaves fresh sage
1/4 lb (115 g) sole fillet, cut in pieces
3 eggs
1/2 cup (125 mL) grated Parmigiano Reggiano
1 clove garlic, peeled
3 Tbsp (45 mL) finely chopped flat-leaf parsley
3 Tbsp (45 mL) finely chopped fresh chives
3 Tbsp (45 mL) finely chopped fresh basil
1 Tbsp (15 mL) finely chopped fresh marjoram
Salt and pepper
8 breadsticks or toasted diagonal baguette slices brushed with olive oil

**1** In a saucepan, bring the chicken broth and sage to a boil. Remove from the heat and let steep for about 5 minutes. Remove and discard the sage.

**2** In a food processor, purée the fish, eggs, Parmigiano and garlic.

**3** Pour the fish mixture into the broth. Bring to a boil while whisking constantly. Add the herbs. Season with salt and pepper.

**4** Serve with breadsticks or toasted baguette slices.

YUM!

# CHICKEN LEGS WITH HONEY AND ROSEMARY

*Preparation* 15 MINUTES          *Cooking* 30 TO 45 MINUTES          *Serves* 8

8 chicken legs
16 large sheets heavy-duty foil
8 sprigs fresh rosemary
1/2 cup (125 mL) honey
Salt and pepper

**1** Preheat the barbecue, setting the burners to high, or place the oven rack in the middle position and preheat to 400°F (200°C).
**2** Place a chicken leg on 2 stacked sheets of foil. Top with a rosemary sprig and drizzle with honey. Season with salt and pepper. Lift the edges of the sheets and crimp them together to form a tightly sealed packet. Grill until the chicken is cooked through and the meat falls easily from the bone, about 15 minutes per side. If using the oven method, arrange the chicken (not wrapped in foil) on a baking sheet and cook for about 45 minutes.

# 3 ingredients

# PASTA WITH PUTTANESCA SAUCE

*Preparation* 10 MINUTES     *Cooking* 10 MINUTES     *Serves* 4

1 onion, chopped
3 cloves garlic, chopped
1/4 cup (60 mL) olive oil
2 anchovy fillets, finely sliced (optional)
3 cups (750 mL) homemade or store-bought tomato sauce
1/4 cup (60 mL) fresh parsley, finely chopped
1/3 cup (75 mL) oil-packed black olives, drained, pitted and halved
2 Tbsp (30 mL) capers, drained and chopped
2 Tbsp (30 mL) fresh oregano, finely chopped
Salt and pepper
3/4 lb (350 g) pasta, cooked

**1** In a saucepan over medium heat, soften the onion and garlic in the oil. Add the anchovies and stir for 1 minute. Add the tomato sauce and bring to a boil. Simmer for 5 minutes. Add the remaining ingredients. Season with salt and pepper. Toss with cooked pasta.

# 5-MINUTE COCONUT-MILK FISH

*Preparation* 15 MINUTES     *Cooking* 5 MINUTES     *Serves* 4

1-1/2 lb (675 g) basa (pangasius) fillets, cubed
14 oz (398 mL) can coconut milk
2 Tbsp (30 mL) finely chopped fresh ginger
1/4 tsp (1.25 mL) ground coriander
Grated zest and juice of 1 lime
Salt and pepper

**1** In a saucepan, combine all the ingredients except the lime juice. Season with salt and pepper. Bring to a boil, reduce the heat, cover and simmer gently for about 5 minutes. Add lime juice to taste. Adjust the seasoning.
**2** Serve on a bed of steamed jasmine rice and accompany with green vegetables and lime wedges.

# LEMON AND GARLIC SHRIMP KEBABS

*Preparation* 10 MINUTES        *Cooking* 7 MINUTES        *Serves* 4

**It's official: a quick visit has become a full-blown dinner. Run to the freezer, grab some shrimp, and drop the bag in cold water right away. Half an hour later—not even enough time for a cocktail—you'll be ready to rock.**

2 lb (1 kg) large raw shrimp, peeled and deveined
Grated zest of 2 lemons
Juice of 1 lemon
2 cloves garlic, minced
3 Tbsp (45 mL) olive oil
Pinch cayenne pepper
Salt and pepper
12 wood skewers, soaked in water for 30 minutes
1 lemon, cut in 6 wedges

**1** In a bowl, toss the shrimp with the lemon zest and juice, garlic, oil and cayenne. Thread the shrimp on the skewers.
**2** Refrigerate for at least 10 minutes, longer if possible.
**3** Preheat the barbecue, setting the burners to high, or preheat a non-stick grill pan.
**4** Season the kebabs with salt and pepper. Grill for 1 to 2 minutes per side, depending on the size. Serve with the lemon wedges.

# FLAMBÉED MORELLO CHERRIES

*Preparation* 5 MINUTES        *Cooking* 5 MINUTES        *Serves* 4

**When I was a kid, the only cherries I knew came in jars. They were either red or green—and always rubbery. Then, one day, I discovered morello cherries. What a revelation! Since that day, I've always kept a jar in the pantry. I add a little rum, some sugar and some butter, then flambé them before serving with ice cream. Ready in a snap.**

1 Tbsp (15 mL) butter
19 oz (540 mL) jar morello cherries or Bing cherries, drained
1 Tbsp (15 mL) sugar
2 Tbsp (30 mL) dark rum
Vanilla ice cream

**1** Melt the butter in a skillet. Sauté the cherries and sugar in the butter over high heat for 2 minutes. Add the rum and flambé immediately. Reduce for 1 minute.
**2** Serve hot over the ice cream.

# RISOTTO À LA WHATEVER

*Preparation* 10 MINUTES          *Cooking* 30 MINUTES          *Serves* 6

Bless the Italian cook who invented this amazing dish! I don't know how many times risotto has saved my life. Rice, onions, broth, wine, Parmesan: these are ingredients that we almost always have on hand. The beauty of this basic recipe is that you can easily jazz it up by cooking an additional ingredient and adding it to the finished risotto: frozen peas, sautéed mushrooms, cooked asparagus, grilled or broiled shrimp with lemon zest ... to name just a few. If you've got an impatient guest, hand over your wooden spoon and get some help with all that stirring!

1 small onion, finely chopped
1/4 cup (60 mL) butter
2 cups (500 mL) arborio, carnaroli or vialone nano rice
1/2 cup (125 mL) white wine
4-1/2 cups (1.125 L) hot chicken broth (approx)
1-1/2 cups (375 mL) grated Parmigiano Reggiano
Salt and pepper

**1** In a saucepan over medium heat, soften the onion in the butter. Add the rice and cook for 1 minute, stirring to coat thoroughly with butter. Add the wine and reduce until almost dry.
**2** Add 1/2 cup (125 mL) of broth at a time, stirring constantly until each addition of broth is almost entirely absorbed. Repeat until all the broth is used and the rice is tender.
**3** Remove from the heat. Add the Parmigiano and stir until melted. Adjust the seasoning. Stir in your choice of additional ingredients. Serve immediately.

PRACTICAL

# CREAM-FREE PENNE ROMANOFF

*Preparation* 20 MINUTES          *Cooking* 25 MINUTES          *Serves* 6

My friend Guy is always trying to tell me how great his healthy recipes taste.
I'll never admit it to him, but I've fallen for his penne. Here's the recipe.

### Béchamel
3 Tbsp (45 mL) butter
3 Tbsp (45 mL) flour
1-1/2 cups (375 mL) milk
Salt and pepper

### Pasta
1 lb (500 g) penne rigate
1 lb (500 g) small white button mushrooms, quartered
3 Tbsp (45 mL) butter
3 green onions, finely sliced
2 cloves garlic, finely chopped
Freshly crushed peppercorns
1/2 cup (125 mL) vodka
1 cup (250 mL) canned diced plum tomatoes, drained

### Garnish
1 cup (250 mL) grated Parmigiano Reggiano
2 green onions, sliced
1/4 cup (60 mL) toasted pine nuts

**1 BÉCHAMEL** Melt the butter in a saucepan. Add the flour and stir for 1 minute. Gradually whisk in the milk. Bring to a boil while whisking constantly, then lower the heat and simmer gently for a few minutes. Season with salt and pepper.

**2 PASTA** Cook the pasta in a large pot of boiling salted water until al dente. Drain, oil lightly, and set aside.

**3** In a large skillet over high heat, sauté the mushrooms in the butter until they release their liquid and brown. Season with salt and pepper. Add the onions and garlic. Continue cooking for about 2 minutes. Add the pasta and crushed pepper and heat through. Deglaze with the vodka, flambéing if desired. Add the béchamel and tomatoes and stir to coat the pasta. Adjust the seasoning. Transfer to a large serving bowl.

**4 GARNISH** Garnish with the Parmigiano, green onions and pine nuts.

# MINESTRONE

*Preparation* 15 MINUTES        *Cooking* 25 MINUTES        *Serves* 4

**Even if you simply pull it out of the freezer, your guests will never know!**

1 onion, chopped
2 carrots, diced
2 stalks celery, diced
2 cloves garlic, chopped
2 Tbsp (30 mL) olive oil
5 cups (1.25 L) chicken broth
1 piece Parmigiano Reggiano rind
1 thick slice prosciutto (optional)
1 zucchini, diced
1 cup (250 mL) green beans, cut in 1-inch (2.5 cm) lengths
1 cup (250 mL) cherry tomatoes, halved
19 oz (540 mL) can red kidney beans, rinsed and drained
1/2 cup (125 mL) grated Parmigiano Reggiano
Chopped fresh basil
Salt and pepper

**1** In a stock pot, sauté the onion, carrots, celery and garlic in the oil. Add the broth, Parmigiano rind and prosciutto.
**2** Bring to a boil, reduce the heat and simmer until the carrots are tender, about 10 minutes.
**3** Add the zucchini, green beans, cherry tomatoes and kidney beans. Simmer for 5 to 7 minutes. Remove the Parmigiano rind and prosciutto. Adjust the seasoning.
**4** Sprinkle with Parmigiano and basil.

# SUN-DRIED TOMATO AND PUMPKIN SEED PESTO

*Preparation* 10 MINUTES    *Serves* 4

1/2 cup (125 mL) oil-packed sun-dried tomatoes, drained and finely chopped
1/4 cup (60 mL) pumpkin seeds, toasted and chopped
1 Tbsp (15 mL) capers, chopped
1/3 cup (75 mL) olive oil

**1** In a bowl, combine the tomatoes, pumpkin seeds, capers and oil.
**2** Serve at room temperature over the cod on page 073, toasted bread slices (bruschetta), in a vinaigrette or with pasta.

# COD WITH SUN-DRIED TOMATO AND PUMPKIN SEED PESTO

*Preparation* 20 MINUTES          *Cooking* 15 MINUTES          *Serves* 4

1 recipe Sun-dried Tomato and Pumpkin Seed Pesto (page 070)

*Zucchini*
1/2 cup (125 mL) chicken broth
3 Tbsp (45 mL) butter
4 zucchini, sliced lengthwise into ribbons with a mandoline
4 leaves fresh sage or basil, finely chopped
Salt and pepper

*Cod*
1-1/4 lb (675 g) cod or whitefish fillets
2 Tbsp (30 mL) olive oil

**1 ZUCCHINI** In a large skillet, bring the broth and butter to a boil and reduce by half. Add the zucchini and the sage or basil. Continue cooking, stirring gently, until the zucchini is just tender, 3 to 4 minutes. Season with salt and pepper. Keep warm.
**2 COD** In the same skillet, brown the fish in the oil over medium heat, 3 to 4 minutes per side. Season with salt and pepper.
**3** Serve the fish topped with the pesto and accompanied by the zucchini.

# CRISPY SHREDDED WHEAT™ FISH FILLETS

*Preparation* 25 MINUTES      *Cooking* 15 MINUTES      *Serves* 4

### Tomato sauce
1 clove garlic, chopped
1 Tbsp (15 mL) olive oil
14 oz (398 mL) can plum tomatoes
3 Tbsp (45 mL) orange juice (optional)
1 tsp (5 mL) honey
Salt and pepper

or

### Tartar sauce
1/2 cup (125 mL) mayonnaise
1 Tbsp (15 mL) chopped sweet pickles
1 Tbsp (15 mL) lime juice
1 tsp (5 mL) chopped capers
1 tsp (5 mL) finely chopped fresh chives

### Fish
1/2 cup (125 mL) unbleached all-purpose flour
3 eggs, lightly beaten
2 cups (500 mL) crumbled Shredded Wheat™
Four 6 oz (170 g) whitefish fillets (basa, tilapia, etc.)
1/4 cup (60 mL) olive oil (approx)

**1 TOMATO SAUCE**  In a small saucepan over medium heat, soften the garlic in the oil for 1 minute. Add the tomatoes, orange juice (if using) and honey. Bring to a boil, reduce the heat and simmer gently for 15 minutes. Season with salt and pepper. Purée the sauce in a blender. Adjust the seasoning. Keep warm.
**2 TARTAR SAUCE**  Combine all the ingredients in a bowl. Season with salt and pepper.
**3 FISH**  Put the flour in one bowl, the beaten eggs in a second bowl and the cereal in a third bowl.
**4** Cut each fillet lengthwise in two. Season with salt and pepper. Dip the fillets in the flour, then in the eggs. Shake off the excess then coat with the cereal crumbs. In a skillet over medium heat, brown the fillets in oil for 2 to 3 minutes per side. Season with salt. Serve with your choice of sauce and a green salad.

# MACARONI AND CHEESE

*Preparation* 20 MINUTES     *Cooking* 20 MINUTES     *Serves* 4 (MAIN COURSE) OR 8 (APPETIZER)

3/4 lb (350 g) elbow macaroni
3 Tbsp (45 mL) butter
3 Tbsp (45 mL) unbleached all-purpose flour
1/2 tsp (2.5 mL) paprika
1/4 tsp (1.25 mL) dried mustard
Pinch ground nutmeg
1-3/4 cups (430 mL) milk
1-1/2 cups (375 mL) grated sharp cheddar (about 5 oz/150 g)
1/4 tsp (1.25 mL) Tabasco sauce or to taste
Salt and pepper

### *Topping (optional)*
5 slices bacon
1-1/2 cups (375 mL) diced bread
3 Tbsp (45 mL) butter

**1** Cook the macaroni in a large pot of boiling salted water until al dente. Drain and coat lightly with oil. Set aside.

**2** Melt the butter in the same pot. Add the flour, paprika, mustard and nutmeg and continue cooking for 1 minute, stirring constantly. Slowly whisk in the milk. Bring to a boil, stirring constantly. Simmer for 2 minutes. Add the cheddar and stir until melted. Season with salt and pepper. Add the macaroni and Tabasco sauce. Adjust the seasoning. If necessary, thin with a small amount of milk.

**3 TOPPING** Meanwhile, fry the bacon in a skillet until crisp. Drain on paper towels. Crumble into small pieces.

**4** In the same skillet, brown the diced bread in the butter and add the bacon.

**5** Top each serving with bacon and croutons. Season with pepper.

# SPINACH POLPETTI WITH TOMATO SAUCE

*Preparation* 30 MINUTES     *Cooking* 20 MINUTES     *Serves* 4

**Polpetti. What a funny name! I didn't really know what they were all about until Étienne, one of the cooks on my team, insisted that I give them a try. Now I just can't get enough of these Italian spinach balls. You've got to taste them for yourself.**

## Tomato sauce
1 small onion, chopped
2 cloves garlic, chopped
1/4 cup (60 mL) olive oil
19 oz (540 mL) can crushed plum tomatoes
Salt and pepper

## Polpetti
6 oz (170 g) bag fresh spinach or 3/4 cup (180 mL) frozen spinach, thawed and drained
1/4 cup (60 mL) olive oil
2 cloves garlic, peeled and halved
1 lb (500 g) ricotta
1/2 cup (125 mL) grated Parmigiano Reggiano
2 eggs
3/4 cup (180 mL) unbleached all-purpose flour
Parmigiano Reggiano shavings to taste
Fresh basil leaves to taste

**1 TOMATO SAUCE** In a saucepan over medium heat, soften the onion and garlic in the olive oil. Add the tomatoes. Bring to a boil, reduce the heat, and simmer for about 10 minutes. Season with salt and pepper. Keep warm.

**2 POLPETTI** In a large skillet over medium-high heat, wilt the spinach in the oil. Transfer to a sieve, drain well and let cool.

**3** In a food processor, purée the spinach, garlic, ricotta, grated Parmigiano and eggs. Add the flour and mix well. Season with salt and pepper.

**4** Using 2 soup spoons, shape about 2 Tbsp (30 mL) of dough into an oval dumpling. Repeat until all the dough is used up. Drop the dumplings, about 10 at a time, into a saucepan of salted simmering water. Cook for 5 or 6 minutes. Drain and coat lightly with oil. Transfer to a plate and keep warm.

**5** Transfer the sauce to a large, shallow serving bowl. Set the dumplings on the sauce. Garnish with Parmigiano shavings and basil leaves. Season with pepper.

# PORK TENDERLOINS WITH BACON BREADING

**Preparation** 15 MINUTES          **Cooking** 25 MINUTES          **Serves** 4 TO 6

3 slices bacon, individually frozen and cut in small pieces
1/2 cup (125 mL) breadcrumbs, preferably homemade
2 Tbsp (30 mL) finely chopped fresh chives
2 Tbsp (30 mL) Dijon mustard
1 Tbsp (15 mL) honey
2 pork tenderloins
Salt and pepper

**1** With the rack in the middle position, preheat the oven to 400°F (200°C). Line a baking sheet with foil or parchment paper.
**2** In a food processor, chop the bacon pieces into small bits. Add the breadcrumbs and chives and pulse for a few seconds. Set aside on a plate.
**3** In a bowl, combine the mustard and honey. Set aside.
**4** Brush the meat with the mustard mixture. Season with salt and pepper. Roll the tenderloins in the breadcrumb mixture, pressing firmly. Bake until the meat is light pink, 20 to 25 minutes depending on thickness. Brown under the broiler if necessary. Let rest for 5 minutes.
**5** Slice thinly. Serve with green vegetables and Vanilla-Pink Peppercorn Potato Purée (facing page).

# VANILLA-PINK PEPPERCORN POTATO PURÉE

*Preparation* 15 MINUTES    *Cooking* 15 MINUTES    *Serves* 4

1 vanilla bean
1/2 cup (125 mL) milk (approx)
4 cups (1 L) peeled and cubed potatoes
1/4 cup (60 mL) butter
2 Tbsp (30 mL) crushed pink peppercorns
Salt

**1** With the tip of a knife, split the vanilla bean lengthwise and scrape out the seeds.
**2** In a saucepan, gently heat the milk with the vanilla seeds and pod until the milk is hot but not boiling. Remove the vanilla pod.
**3** Meanwhile, in a saucepan, boil the potatoes in salted water until tender, about 15 minutes. Drain.
**4** Mash the potatoes with the butter. Add the milk and peppercorns and purée using an electric mixer. Adjust the seasoning.

# QUICK RASPBERRY MOUSSE

*Preparation* 20 MINUTES      *Serves* 6 TO 8

**There are a thousand and one ways to make a mousse. You know me: I went with the easiest one. With just four ingredients, you'll get a flavour explosion. You can also use frozen raspberries; just defrost and drain them first.**

3 egg whites
1/4 tsp (1 mL) cream of tartar
1 cup (250 mL) sugar
2-1/2 cups (625 mL) fresh raspberries
Thin cookies

**1** In a bowl, beat the egg whites and cream of tartar with an electric mixer until soft peaks form. Gradually add the sugar, beating until the peaks are very stiff, about 6 minutes. Add 1-1/2 cups (375 mL) raspberries and continue beating for 1 minute. Refrigerate.
**2** To serve, spoon the mousse into 6 dessert cups. Garnish with the remaining fresh raspberries and the cookies. The mousse can be made several hours before serving. If necessary, beat it again to restore its velvety texture.

RECIPE P084

# MINI TARTE TATIN

*Preparation* 15 MINUTES     *Cooking* 35 MINUTES     *Serves* 6

**You don't need a special pan to make these upside-down tartlets; all it takes is a six-cup muffin pan. Are the apples stuck to the bottom? Don't panic, just loosen them with a spoon. And feel free to try this recipe with pears.**

1/4 lb (115 g) store-bought puff pastry dough, thawed but still cold
1/2 cup (125 mL) water
1 cup (250 mL) sugar
4 Royal Gala or Cortland apples, peeled, cored and cut in 1/2-inch (1 cm) dice

**1** With the rack in the middle position, preheat the oven to 400°F (200°C). Generously butter a 6-cup muffin pan.
**2** Roll out the pastry to a thickness of about 1/8 inch (3 mm). Using a pastry cutter the same diameter as the muffin cups, cut 6 circles. Place the circles on a baking sheet and refrigerate.
**3** In a skillet, bring the water and sugar to a boil. Cook over high heat until the sugar starts to brown. Add the apples and simmer for 5 to 8 minutes, stirring frequently.
**4** Divide the apples and syrup among the muffin cups. Place on a baking sheet in case the syrup spills over. Cover the apples with the pastry. Bake until golden brown, 15 to 20 minutes.
**5** Line a baking sheet with parchment paper. Let the tartlets cool for 2 minutes, then unmould onto the baking sheet. Serve warm or cold.

# VANILLA ICING

*Preparation* 10 MINUTES      *Makes* 4 CUPS (1 L)

**This icing transforms a simple vanilla cake into an elegant dessert.**

1-3/4 cups (430 mL) unsalted butter, softened
3-1/2 cups (875 mL) icing sugar
1/2 cup (125 mL) heavy cream (35%)
1 tsp (5 mL) vanilla extract
1/4 tsp (1 mL) salt
1/2 cup (125 mL) boiling water

**1** Using an electric mixer or stand mixer, beat the butter, sugar, cream, vanilla and salt until frothy and smooth, about 2 minutes. Add the boiling water 1 Tbsp (15 mL) at a time, beating for 30 seconds between additions. Spread about 3/4 cup (180 mL) of icing between each layer of a cake and about 1-3/4 cups (430 mL) over the top and sides (see Perfect Vanilla Cake, page 086).

**Other finishing touches for Perfect Vanilla Cake:**

Strawberry coulis (page 089)
Caramel sauce (page 218)
Quick strawberry–maple syrup jam (page 027)
Chocolate sauce (page 213)
Mascarpone cream (page 183)
Cranberry compote (page 122)

# PERFECT VANILLA CAKE

*Preparation* 35 MINUTES          *Cooking* 55 MINUTES          *Resting time* 3 HOURS          *Serves* 12

**Friends showing up any minute? This versatile cake can easily become short-cake, jam cake or even, with the Vanilla Icing on page 085, a great birthday cake.**

3-1/4 cups (810 mL) unbleached all-purpose flour
1 Tbsp (15 mL) baking powder
1/2 tsp (2.5 mL) salt
4 eggs
2 cups (500 mL) sugar
1 tsp (5 mL) vanilla extract
3/4 cup (180 mL) canola oil
1-1/4 cups (310 mL) milk

**1** With the rack in the middle position, preheat the oven to 350°F (180°C). Line two 8-inch (20 cm) springform pans with parchment paper and butter the paper. Set aside.
**2** In a bowl, combine the flour, baking powder and salt. Set aside.
**3** In another bowl, beat the eggs, sugar and vanilla using an electric mixer until the mixture turns pale, doubles in volume and falls from the beaters in ribbons, about 10 minutes. With the mixer running, add the oil in a thin stream.
**4** With the mixer on low, add the dry ingredients, alternating with the milk, until the batter is smooth. Pour into the 2 pans and bake until a toothpick inserted in the centre comes out clean, 50 to 55 minutes. Let cool for 15 minutes. Unmould and cool completely (about 2 to 3 hours) on a rack.
**5** Place the cakes on a clean surface. Cut a thin slice off the top to flatten them. Slice each cake in half horizontally before icing (see page 85).

WHiPPED CReAM

or

NUTELLA

or

berries OR

strawberry jam

# STRAWBERRY AND BALSAMIC VINEGAR SUNDAES

*Preparation* 20 MINUTES    *Cooking* 20 MINUTES    *Serves* 6

### Strawberry coulis
3 cups (750 mL) fresh strawberries, hulled and halved
1/3 cup (75 mL) sugar

### Balsamic vinegar syrup
1/3 cup (75 mL) maple syrup
1/3 cup (75 mL) balsamic vinegar

### Sundaes
24 fresh strawberries, sliced
1/2 cup (125 mL) heavy cream (35%)
1 Tbsp (15 mL) sugar
4 cups (1 L) vanilla ice cream

**1 STRAWBERRY COULIS**  In a saucepan, combine the strawberries and sugar. Bring to a boil over medium heat, stirring frequently. Reduce the heat and simmer for 6 to 8 minutes. Purée in a blender. Strain and let stand until lukewarm. Cover and refrigerate for 1-1/2 hours. To cool more quickly, place the coulis in the freezer, stirring frequently, until it reaches room temperature. Add the sliced strawberries and mix well. Set aside.

**2 BALSAMIC VINEGAR SYRUP**  Bring the maple syrup and vinegar to a boil in a saucepan. Cook until a candy thermometer reads 225°F (110°C), about 5 minutes. Remove from the heat and pour the syrup into a bowl. Let cool, then cover.

**3 SUNDAES**  In a bowl, whip the cream with the sugar. Refrigerate.

**4** Spoon half the strawberry mixture into 6 sundae glasses, add a scoop of ice cream to each glass, then drizzle with balsamic vinegar syrup. Add another scoop of ice cream, spoon in the remaining strawberry mixture and top with dollops of whipped cream. Drizzle with balsamic vinegar syrup.

Whether they'll admit it or not, visitors who come to Canada from Europe are looking for "wilderness," both in what they see and what they eat. To impress them (while having a few good-natured laughs), I like to let my culinary imagination run ... wild! I serve them "wild" duck, "wild" sausages, "wild" sliced bread. The same goes for service—I trade in my butter dish for a bed of spruce branches, and pass the cheese around on a snowshoe strung with rawhide. And because our friends are eager to learn, I like to teach them about the difference between "wild" and "farmed" maple syrup. Of course, it's the exact same thing, but when I challenge them to taste the "wild" stuff, they're sure to notice the difference right away. It gives them yet another way to impress their friends back home. Of course, I always sing the praises of wild Rocky Mountain corn on the cob. You know, the kind that hockey players harvest on snowshoeing expeditions every fall. Or sometimes I'll just serve fresh, tasty local products. It's not as funny, but it's more fun all around.

# entertaining European guests in summer

# CRAB AND STRAWBERRY SALAD WITH LIME

*Preparation* 10 MINUTES        *Serves* 4 TO 6

**Spring is the season for snow crab from the Gaspé and the Lower St. Lawrence. The rest of the year, you can buy it in frozen pieces. For a change of pace, you can also make this recipe with lobster or fresh shrimp. The key is the subtle flavour of the sea.**

Flesh of 2 avocados, cut in 1-inch (2.5 cm) cubes
1 English cucumber, peeled, seeded and cut in 1-inch (2.5 cm) cubes
1-1/2 cups (375 mL) fresh strawberries, quartered
3/4 lb (350 g) snow crab meat
Juice of 2 limes
3 Tbsp (45 mL) olive oil
Salt and pepper

**1** In a bowl, gently toss all the ingredients. Season with salt and pepper.
**2** Serve immediately.

# ASPARAGUS CAESAR SALAD

*Preparation* 30 MINUTES          *Cooking* 20 MINUTES          *Serves* 4 TO 6

### *Dressing*
1 egg yolk
1 Tbsp (15 mL) lemon juice
2 tsp (10 mL) Dijon mustard
1 tsp (5 mL) chopped capers
1/2 tsp (2.5 mL) anchovy paste or 1 chopped anchovy fillet
1/2 cup (125 mL) vegetable oil
Salt and pepper

### *Salad*
2 slices bread, cut in 1/4-inch (0.5 cm) cubes
2 Tbsp (30 mL) butter (approx)
1/2 lb (225 g) bacon, cut in small pieces
2 lb (1 kg) asparagus, trimmed
Grated zest of 1 lemon
Parmigiano Reggiano shavings to taste

**1 DRESSING**  In a bowl, whisk together the egg yolk, lemon juice, mustard, capers and anchovy paste. Add the oil in a thin stream, whisking constantly. Season with salt and pepper.
**2 SALAD**  In a skillet, brown the bread in the butter. Set aside on a plate.
**3** In the same skillet, fry the bacon until crisp. Drain on paper towels.
**4** Boil the asparagus in salted water until al dente, about 3 minutes. Drain.
**5** In a bowl, toss the asparagus, lemon zest and bacon. Transfer to a plate.
**6** Pour the dressing over the asparagus in a thin stream. Sprinkle with croutons and Parmigiano shavings. Serve as an appetizer or as a side dish.

# GRILLED HALIBUT WITH HERBES SALÉES SALSA VERDE

*Preparation* 10 MINUTES    *Cooking* 20 MINUTES    *Serves* 4

### Grilled halibut
1 piece skinless halibut fillet, 2 lb (1 kg)
Olive oil
Salt and pepper

### Salsa verde
1 cup (250 mL) olive oil
1 cup (250 mL) fresh flat-leaf parsley
1/2 cup (125 mL) fresh basil
2 green onions, sliced in short lengths
2 Tbsp (30 mL) *herbes salées* (recipe follows)
1 tsp (5 mL) fresh thyme

**1 GRILLED HALIBUT** Preheat the barbecue, setting the burners to high.
**2** Brush the halibut on both sides with olive oil. Season with salt and pepper. Place on a sheet of foil. Grill for 15 to 20 minutes.
**3 SALSA VERDE** Place all the ingredients in a blender and purée until smooth. Serve with the grilled halibut.

# HERBES SALÉES

*Preparation* 30 MINUTES    *Refrigeration* 4 TO 5 DAYS    *Makes* 4 CUPS (1 L)

**Herbes salées (herbs preserved with salt) are a traditional Quebec seasoning. Often used to flavour soups, they can also be added to mashed potatoes, salad dressings and any dish that will be enhanced by the pleasing taste of salty fresh herbs.**

1-1/2 cups (375 mL) fresh parsley leaves
1/4 cup (60 mL) fresh chives
1/4 cup (60 mL) fresh summer savoury leaves
2 tsp (10 mL) fresh thyme leaves
1 tsp (5 mL) fresh rosemary leaves
1-1/2 cups (375 mL) finely diced carrots
1-1/2 cups (375 mL) finely chopped leeks (white and green parts)
1/2 cup (125 mL) finely chopped celery
4 green onions, finely chopped
3/4 cup (180 mL) coarse salt

**1** Finely chop all the herbs.
**2** Combine all the ingredients in a glass bowl. Cover and refrigerate for 4 to 5 days.
**3** Spoon into eight 1/2-cup (125 mL) jars. Seal and refrigerate. The herbs will keep for at least several weeks in the refrigerator.

BROWN TARRAGON BUTTER P104

DOMINO NEUVILLE

LEMON-LIME BUTTER P104

BACON-MUSTARD BUTTER P104

# BACON-MUSTARD BUTTER

*Preparation* 10 MINUTES    *Cooking* 5 MINUTES    *Refrigeration* 20 MINUTES
*Makes* 2/3 CUP (150 ML)

3 slices bacon, coarsely chopped
2 tsp (10 mL) whole-grain mustard
1/2 cup (125 mL) salted butter, softened

**1** Brown the bacon in a skillet. Drain on paper towels and let cool.
**2** In a food processor or using a knife, chop the bacon into small bits. Add the mustard and butter and mix well. Transfer to a ramekin and refrigerate for about 20 minutes.
**3** Serve with corn on the cob, steak or grilled chicken.

# LEMON-LIME BUTTER

*Preparation* 10 MINUTES    *Refrigeration* 20 MINUTES    *Makes* 2/3 CUP (150 ML)

1/2 cup (125 mL) salted butter, softened
Grated zest of 1/2 lemon
Grated zest of 1 lime
1 Tbsp (15 mL) lemon juice
1 Tbsp (15 mL) lime juice

**1** Place all ingredients in a bowl or a small food processor and mix well. Transfer to a ramekin and refrigerate for 20 minutes.
**2** Serve with corn on the cob or grilled fish.

# BROWN TARRAGON BUTTER

*Preparation* 10 MINUTES    *Cooking* 5 MINUTES    *Refrigeration* 20 MINUTES
*Makes* 1/2 CUP (125 ML)

1/2 cup (125 mL) butter, softened
1 tsp (5 mL) white wine vinegar
2 tsp (10 mL) fresh tarragon, finely chopped
Pepper

**1** Place 3 Tbsp (45 mL) butter and the vinegar in a small skillet and slowly bring to a boil. Cook until the butter turns nut-brown. Pour into a bowl immediately to stop the cooking. Let cool until lukewarm, about 15 minutes.
**2** Place the remaining butter, the browned butter and the tarragon in a bowl or a small food processor and mix well. Transfer to a ramekin and refrigerate for about 20 minutes.
**3** Serve with corn on the cob, fish, asparagus or grilled chicken.

ETTES DE POULET
'9 MORCEAUX
'20 MORCEAUX
CROQUETTES GARNIES +
OIGNONS FRANCAIS
POUTINE  RÉGULIÈRE
                GROSSE
            FAMILIALE
POUTINE ITALIENNE REG.
                GROSSE
            FAMILIALE
GALVAUDE RÉGULIÈRE
            GROSSE
            FAMILIALE

3.95
5.20
8.75
2.05
3.95
4.90
6.95
10.50
5.80
7.95
13.00
4.90
6.95
10.50

# AMERICAN-STYLE DOUBLE CHEESEBURGERS

*Preparation* 20 MINUTES          *Cooking* 10 MINUTES          *Serves* 4

### Sauce

3/4 cup (180 mL) mayonnaise
1/4 cup (60 mL) finely chopped onion
1 Tbsp (15 mL) store-bought French salad dressing (orange coloured)
1 Tbsp (15 mL) sweet relish
1 Tbsp (15 mL) finely chopped dill pickle
1 tsp (5 mL) brown sugar
1 tsp (5 mL) ketchup
1 tsp (5 mL) white vinegar
Salt and pepper

### Cheeseburgers

4 hamburger buns
1-1/2 lb (675 g) lean ground beef
4 slices orange processed cheese
Sliced sandwich pickles
Chopped iceberg lettuce

**1 SAUCE**  In a bowl, combine all the ingredients. Season with salt and pepper. Refrigerate.

**2 CHEESEBURGERS**  Preheat the barbecue, setting the burners to high.

**3** Using a bread knife, slice the top halves of the hamburger buns in half. Set aside.

**4** Shape the meat into 8 large but very thin patties. Tip: place the patties between sheets of plastic wrap and flatten by sliding your hand over the top layer.

**5** Grill the patties until well-done, about 3 minutes per side. Season with salt and pepper. Place the cheese slices on 4 of the patties for the last minute of cooking. Toast the buns.

**6 ASSEMBLY**  Spread sauce on the bun bottoms. Lay 1 plain patty on each bun bottom. Garnish with pickle slices. Cover with the bun middles. Spread with sauce and garnish with lettuce. Top with the remaining patties and the bun tops.

RECIPE P114

# MINI PO' BOY SANDWICHES

*Preparation* 20 MINUTES     *Cooking* 7 MINUTES     *Serves* 8

The po' boy is a New Orleans invention: a submarine sandwich loaded with fried oysters, crayfish or crab topped with lettuce, pickles, tomatoes and mayonnaise. It's simple fare, ideal for lunch with corn on the cob.

### *Tartar sauce*

1/2 cup (125 mL) mayonnaise
1/4 cup (60 mL) finely chopped sour pickles
1 Tbsp (15 mL) lemon juice
1 tsp (5 mL) creamed prepared horseradish
1/4 tsp (1 mL) sugar
Salt and pepper

### *Fried oysters*

1-1/2 cups (375 mL) fine cornmeal
1/2 tsp (2.5 mL) cayenne pepper
3/4 lb (350 g) shucked oysters, drained and patted dry

### *Sandwiches*

1 baguette (or 4 small submarine buns), halved lengthwise
1 cup (250 mL) iceberg lettuce, thinly sliced
1 tomato, thinly sliced

**1 TARTAR SAUCE** In a bowl, combine all the ingredients. Season with salt and pepper. Refrigerate.
**2 FRIED OYSTERS** Preheat the oil in the deep-fryer to 350°F (180°C). Line a baking sheet with several layers of paper towels.
**3** With the oven rack in the middle position, preheat the broiler.
**4** In a bowl, combine the cornmeal and cayenne. Season with salt. Dredge the oysters in the cornmeal mixture, coating them well.
**5** Drop half the oysters into the deep-fryer and fry until golden, 1 to 2 minutes, depending on size. Drain and transfer to the paper towels. Repeat with the remaining oysters. Season with salt.
**6 SANDWICHES** Meanwhile, toast the bread under the broiler for 2 to 3 minutes.
**7** Spread tartar sauce on each half. Top the bottom half with lettuce, tomatoes and fried oysters. Cover with the top half of the bread and press firmly. Cut into 2-inch (5 cm) pieces and insert a toothpick in each bite.
**8** Serve as an hors d'oeuvre or for lunch.

# MONTREAL STEAK SPICE

*Preparation* 5 MINUTES          *Makes* ABOUT 1/2 CUP (125 ML)

2 Tbsp (30 mL) 4-peppercorn blend
1 Tbsp (15 mL) coriander seeds
1 Tbsp (15 mL) dill seeds
1/2 tsp (2.5 mL) hot pepper flakes
2 Tbsp (30 mL) coarse sea salt
1 Tbsp (15 mL) garlic powder
1 Tbsp (15 mL) onion powder

**1** In a coffee grinder or a mortar, crush the peppercorns, coriander, dill seeds and hot pepper flakes. Add the remaining ingredients and mix well.
**2** Sprinkle generously on steaks (T-bone, filet mignon, etc.), whole chicken before roasting, or tuna steaks before grilling.

# RUSTIC APPLE AND SUMMER BERRY TART

*Preparation* 20 MINUTES     *Refrigeration* 30 MINUTES     *Cooking* 40 MINUTES     *Serves* 10

### Pastry
3 cups (750 mL) unbleached all-purpose flour
Pinch of salt
2 Tbsp (30 mL) sugar
3/4 cup (180 mL) cold unsalted butter, cubed
2 eggs
1/4 cup (60 mL) ice water

### Filling
1 cup (250 mL) sugar
2 Tbsp (30 mL) instant tapioca
4 cups (1 L) mixed berries (cut large strawberries in quarters)
1 Tbsp (15 mL) cornmeal
2 Royal Gala apples, peeled, cored and thinly sliced
Vanilla ice cream

**1 PASTRY** In a food processor, pulse the flour, salt and sugar to combine. Add the butter and pulse briefly until the butter pieces are pea-sized. Add the eggs and water. Pulse until the dough just begins to hold together, adding more water if necessary. Remove the dough from the food processor and shape it into a disc with your hands. Wrap in plastic and refrigerate.

**2** On a floured surface, roll the dough into a disc about 18 inches (46 cm) across.

**3** Move the oven rack to the middle position and place a pizza stone on it. Preheat the oven to 400°F (200°C). If you don't have a pizza stone, use an inverted baking sheet lined with parchment paper but do not place it in the oven before using.

**4 FILLING** In a bowl, combine the sugar and tapioca. Add the berries and toss well. Let rest for 10 minutes.

**5** Dust the pizza stone with cornmeal. Place the dough on it. Cover the centre with apple slices, leaving a 6-inch (15 cm) border. Spoon the berry mixture over the apples and fold in the edge of the dough. If desired, pinch the edge to raise it slightly to prevent the fruit juices from running. Bake until the dough is golden brown, about 40 minutes.

**6** Serve the tart with vanilla ice cream.

RECIPE P122

# BANANA SPLITS WITH CRANBERRY COMPOTE AND COFFEE CARAMEL SAUCE

*Preparation* 20 MINUTES      *Cooking* 20 MINUTES      *Refrigeration* 12 HOURS      *Serves* 4

**Any leftover cranberry compote or caramel sauce will keep for a few weeks—the cranberries in the fridge, the caramel at room temperature. Enjoy them with sundaes, cakes or brownies.**

### Cranberry compote
1-1/2 cups (375 mL) sugar
1 cup (250 mL) water
2 cups (500 mL) fresh or frozen cranberries

### Coffee caramel sauce
1/4 cup (60 mL) water
1-1/2 cups (375 mL) sugar
1/2 cup (125 mL) heavy cream (35%)
1/2 cup (125 mL) espresso or strong coffee
1/4 cup (60 mL) salted butter

### Garnishes
4 bananas, halved lengthwise
Vanilla ice cream
1/3 cup (75 mL) pecans, toasted and coarsely chopped

**1 CRANBERRY COMPOTE** In a saucepan, bring the sugar and water to a boil. Add the cranberries. Bring to a boil. Remove from the heat and let cool partially. Refrigerate for 12 hours.

**2 COFFEE CARAMEL SAUCE** In a saucepan, bring the water and sugar to a boil. Simmer without stirring until the mixture turns light gold, about 3 minutes. Remove from the heat. Whisk in the cream, coffee and butter. Bring to a boil and simmer until the mixture is smooth. Let cool, transfer to an airtight container and refrigerate.

**3** Place the bananas in 4 bowls. Add scoops of ice cream. Drizzle with caramel sauce and top with cranberry compote and pecans.

# BLUEBERRY PUDDING ON THE BARBECUE

**Preparation** 10 MINUTES     **Cooking** 25 MINUTES     **Serves** 8

**Our blueberries have a European cousin known as bilberries, whortleberries or, in France, *myrtilles*. Your European friends will flip for the Canadian kind.**

### Filling

1/2 cup (125 mL) sugar
1/2 tsp (2.5 mL) cornstarch
6 cups (1.5 L) fresh blueberries

### Batter

1-1/4 cups (310 mL) unbleached all-purpose flour
1/2 cup (125 mL) sugar
1 tsp (5 mL) baking powder
1/4 cup (60 mL) unsalted butter, melted
1 cup (250 mL) ginger ale or lemon-lime soft drink (7 Up)

**1** Preheat the barbecue, setting the burners to high.

**2 FILLING** In a bowl, combine the sugar and cornstarch. Add the blueberries and mix well. Spread in an 8-inch (20 cm) square aluminum baking pan. Press gently and set aside.

**3 BATTER** In a bowl, combine the flour, sugar and baking powder. Add the butter in a thin stream and mix. Add the ginger ale and stir with a wooden spoon until the mixture is smooth. Scrape into the baking pan, covering the berries. Set the burners to medium-low. Place the baking pan on the grate and close the lid. Bake until a toothpick inserted in the centre comes out clean, about 30 minutes. To bake in the oven, place the rack in the middle position and preheat to 375°F (190°C). Bake in a Pyrex dish until a toothpick inserted in the centre comes out clean, about 1 hour and 20 minutes.

**4** Let cool for 15 minutes. Serve with vanilla ice cream.

# entertaining European guests in winter

# ONION SOUP WITH BEER

*Preparation* 20 MINUTES        *Cooking* 55 MINUTES        *Serves* 6

10 cups (2.5 L) sliced onions (about 10 medium onions)
1/4 cup (60 mL) butter
1 Tbsp (15 mL) flour
12 oz (341 mL) bottle local pale ale
1 Tbsp (15 mL) Dijon mustard
4 cups (1 L) chicken broth (approx)
6 thick diagonal slices baguette, toasted
2 cups (500 mL) grated sharp cheddar
Salt and pepper

**1** In a large non-stick saucepan over medium-low heat, brown the onions in the butter until golden and soft, about 30 minutes. Season with salt and pepper. Dust with the flour and cook for 1 more minute. Add the beer and mustard and bring to a boil, stirring constantly. Add the broth and bring to a boil. Reduce the heat and simmer for about 10 minutes. Add more broth if necessary. Adjust the seasoning.

**2** With the rack in the middle position, preheat the broiler.

**3** Ladle the soup into 4 ovenproof bowls. Place 1 toast in each bowl and top with cheddar. Place the bowls on a baking sheet. Broil until the cheese is golden brown.

# ATLANTIC TOMCOD MEUNIERE

*Preparation*  15 MINUTES          *Cooking*  15 MINUTES          *Serves*  4 (APPETIZER)

**Fishing for the diminutive tomcod is a tradition on the Sainte-Anne River, in Quebec's Mauricie region. Sitting in cabins perched on the frozen river, the locals harvest the little fish—*Microgadus* tomcod—through small holes cut through the ice. Every January and February, it's a tasty, festive occasion for the whole community.**

12 small tomcod, cleaned and heads removed
3/4 cup (180 mL) unbleached all-purpose flour
1/3 cup (75 mL) butter
Salt and pepper

**1** Thoroughly pat the fish dry with paper towels.
**2** Place the flour in a large bowl. Dredge the fish in the flour, shaking to remove any excess.
**3** In a large non-stick skillet, heat the butter until it foams. Brown the fish on both sides until the bone pulls away easily. Season generously with salt and pepper. Serve immediately, with lemon wedges if desired.

# FISH AND SEAFOOD CHOWDER

*Preparation* 15 MINUTES          *Cooking* 30 MINUTES          *Serves* 4 TO 6

Two 5-1/4 oz (147 g) cans of clams
3 slices bacon, chopped
1 onion, finely chopped
1 cup (250 mL) diced celery
3-1/2 cups (875 mL) chicken broth
4 cups (1 L) peeled and diced potatoes
1-1/2 cups (375 mL) fresh or frozen corn kernels
6 sprigs fresh thyme
1/2 lb (225 g) whitefish fillets (haddock, cod, etc.)
1/2 cup (125 mL) heavy cream (35%)
Fresh chives for garnish
Salt and pepper

**1** Drain the clams, reserving the juice. Set aside.
**2** Brown the bacon in a soup pot over medium heat. Add the onion and celery and soften for a few minutes. Season with salt and pepper. Add the broth, clam juice, potatoes, corn and thyme. Bring to a boil, reduce the heat and simmer until the potatoes are tender, about 20 minutes. Remove the thyme.
**3** Using a blender, purée one-third of the soup and return it to the pot. Add the fish, clams and cream. Bring to a boil and simmer gently until the fish is cooked through. Adjust the seasoning.
**4** Sprinkle with chives.

# SLOW-COOKED BEEF WITH RED WINE

*Preparation* 25 MINUTES    *Cooking* 6 HOURS 15 MINUTES    *Serves* 4 TO 6

**It's easy to forget that a slow cooker makes a great substitute for a camp stove. It's ideal for reheating a winter picnic. Provided, of course, that your destination has access to electricity, you can bring a hot meal almost anywhere—say, a potluck—and delight everyone.**

8 to 12 small new potatoes (or 4 medium potatoes, peeled and halved)
4 carrots, peeled and halved lengthwise
3-1/2 lb (1.6 kg) boneless beef blade roast, cut in 2-inch (5 cm) cubes
2 Tbsp (30 mL) olive oil
2 onions, cut in wedges
4 cloves garlic, peeled and halved
2 Tbsp (30 mL) flour
1 cup (250 mL) red wine
1 cup (250 mL) chicken broth
14 oz (398 mL) can diced tomatoes
3 sprigs fresh thyme
Salt and pepper

**1** Place the potatoes and carrots in the slow cooker.
**2** In a large skillet, brown the meat in the oil. Season with salt and pepper. Place in the slow cooker.
**3** In the same skillet, brown the onions and garlic. Add oil if necessary. Dust with flour and cook for 1 more minute. Add the wine and bring to a boil while stirring. Transfer the mixture to the slow cooker and add the broth, tomatoes and thyme. Cover and cook until the meat is fork tender, about 6 hours with the cooker set to high or 8 hours on low. Remove the thyme. Adjust the seasoning. You can also cook this dish in an oven preheated to 300°F (150°C). Cook for about 4 hours.

# PORK TENDERLOINS GLAZED WITH MAPLE-BEET SAUCE

*Preparation* 15 MINUTES     *Cooking* 30 MINUTES     *Serves* 4

3/4 cup (180 mL) maple syrup
3/4 cup (180 mL) chicken broth
1 medium beet, peeled and diced
1/4 cup (60 mL) Worcestershire sauce
1 Tbsp (15 mL) ground coriander
2 pork tenderloins
1 Tbsp (15 mL) butter
Salt and pepper

**1** With the rack in the middle position, preheat the oven to 350°F (180°C).
**2** In a saucepan, combine the maple syrup, broth, beet and Worcestershire sauce and bring to a boil. Reduce the heat and simmer gently until syrupy, about 20 minutes.
**3** Sprinkle the tenderloins with the coriander. Season with salt and pepper.
**4** In an ovenproof skillet, brown the meat in the butter. Add the sauce, transfer to the oven and roast for about 15 minutes. Remove the skillet from the oven. Transfer the tenderloins to a plate and tent with foil. Reduce the sauce in the skillet over high heat until very syrupy. To serve attractive whole tenderloins, return them to the skillet and turn to coat well.
**5** Cut the tenderloins into thin slices and drizzle with the remaining sauce.
**6** Serve with Celery Roasted with 20 Cloves of Garlic (page 141), Cauliflower Purée (page 141) or Scalloped Jerusalem Artichokes (page 140).

# SCALLOPED JERUSALEM ARTICHOKES

*Preparation* 40 MINUTES        *Cooking* 50 MINUTES        *Serves* 6

I adore Jerusalem artichokes and love getting other people to try them. This tuber, native to North America, is finally getting its due in local cuisine. Its colour, soft skin and irregular shape are reminiscent of fresh ginger. But the similarities end there: it tastes a bit like artichoke, which helps explain the name despite the lack of direct kinship. As soon as you've peeled a Jerusalem artichoke, drop it in water acidified with lemon juice or it will oxidize and blacken quickly.

2 cups (500 mL) heavy cream (35%)
1 egg, lightly beaten
1 clove garlic, finely chopped
1/4 tsp (1 mL) ground nutmeg
2 lb (1 kg) Jerusalem artichokes, peeled and thinly sliced (peeled weight about 1-3/4 lb/750 g)
Salt and pepper

**1** With the rack in the middle position, preheat the oven to 400°F (200°C).
**2** In a bowl, combine the cream, egg, garlic and nutmeg. Add the Jerusalem artichokes. Season with salt and pepper. Transfer to an 8-inch (20 cm) square Pyrex baking dish. Bake until tender, about 50 minutes. Serve as a side dish for pork or beef.

# CAULIFLOWER PURÉE

*Preparation* 10 MINUTES    *Cooking* 20 MINUTES    *Serves* 4 TO 6

1 onion, chopped
1/4 cup (60 mL) butter
1 medium cauliflower, cut in pieces
4 cloves garlic, peeled
3 cups (750 mL) milk
Salt and pepper

**1** In a large saucepan over medium heat, soften the onion in 2 Tbsp (30 mL) butter. Add the cauliflower, garlic and milk. Season with salt and pepper. Bring to a boil. Reduce the heat, cover and simmer gently until the cauliflower is tender, about 15 minutes. Drain well, setting aside the liquid for another use such as cream of cauliflower soup.
**2** In a food processor, purée the cauliflower with about 1/4 cup (60 mL) of the cooking liquid and the remaining butter. Adjust the seasoning.
**3** Serve with pork, beef or chicken.

# CELERY ROASTED WITH 20 CLOVES OF GARLIC

*Preparation* 10 MINUTES    *Cooking* 20 MINUTES    *Serves* 4

8 stalks celery, cut diagonally in 1/2-inch (1 cm) pieces
20 cloves garlic, peeled and halved
2 Tbsp (30 mL) olive oil
*Fleur de sel* or sea salt
2 Tbsp (30 mL) finely chopped celery leaves

**1** With the rack in the middle position, preheat the oven to 350°F (180°C).
**2** Combine the celery, garlic and oil on a rimmed baking sheet. Season with salt. Roast for about 10 minutes, stir, and roast for about 10 more minutes. Sprinkle with chopped celery leaves and adjust the seasoning.
**3** Serve with pork, beef or chicken.

# CHOCOLATE PUDDING

***Preparation*** 30 MINUTES      ***Cooking*** 1 HOUR      ***Serves*** 10

### Sauce

3 cups (750 mL) brown sugar
3/4 cup (180 mL) cocoa powder, sifted
2 tsp (10 mL) cornstarch
2-1/2 cups (625 mL) water
1/2 cup (125 mL) heavy cream (35%)
1/2 tsp (2.5 mL) vanilla extract

### Cake

1 cup (250 mL) milk
1/2 cup (125 mL) cocoa powder, sifted
1-1/2 cups (375 mL) unbleached all-purpose flour
1 tsp (5 mL) baking soda
Pinch salt
1/2 cup (125 mL) unsalted butter, softened
1-1/2 cups (375 mL) sugar
2 eggs

**1** With the rack in the middle position, preheat the oven to 350°F (180°C). Butter a 9- x 13-inch (23 x 33 cm) Pyrex or aluminum baking dish.

**2 SAUCE** In a saucepan, combine the brown sugar, cocoa powder and cornstarch. Add the water and cream. Bring to a boil, whisking constantly. Add the vanilla. Set aside.

**3 CAKE** In a small saucepan, bring the milk and cocoa powder to a boil, whisking constantly. Let cool.

**4** In a bowl, combine the flour, baking soda and salt. Set aside.

**5** In another bowl, cream the butter and sugar with an electric mixer until the mixture resembles coarse sand. Add the eggs and beat until the mixture is smooth. Add the dry ingredients, alternating with the milk mixture. Spread the batter in the baking dish.

**6** Gently pour the hot sauce over the batter. Bake until a toothpick inserted in the centre of the cake comes out clean, about 45 minutes. Serve warm or hot.

# APPLE AND MAPLE VERRINE

*Preparation* 40 MINUTES  *Cooking* 40 MINUTES  *Refrigeration* 4 HOURS  *Serves* 6

This dessert is my take on a pair of Quebec classics: sugar pie and apple crisp, served *en verrine*—in a jar.

### Maple jelly
2 tsp (10 mL) gelatin
1 cup (250 mL) water
3/4 cup (180 mL) maple syrup

### Maple-glazed apples
1/2 cup (125 mL) maple syrup
4 Royal Gala or Cortland apples, peeled, cored and diced

### Crisp
1/2 cup (125 mL) unbleached all-purpose flour
3 Tbsp (45 mL) brown sugar
1/4 tsp (1 mL) salt
1/4 cup (60 mL) unsalted butter, softened

### Whipped cream
1/2 cup (125 mL) heavy cream (35%)
1 Tbsp (15 mL) maple syrup
1/4 cup (60 mL) sour cream

**1 MAPLE JELLY**  In a bowl, sprinkle the gelatin over 1/4 cup (60 mL) water and let soften for 5 minutes. Set aside.

**2** In a saucepan, bring the remaining ingredients to a boil. Add the gelatin and stir until dissolved. Divide the mixture among 6 attractive glasses or small jam jars. Refrigerate for about 4 hours.

**3 MAPLE-GLAZED APPLES**  In a large skillet, bring the maple syrup and apples to a boil. Simmer, stirring frequently, until the apples are tender and the juice syrupy. Let cool partially. Refrigerate until chilled, about 2 hours. Drain the apples.

**4 CRISP**  With the rack in the middle position, preheat the oven to 350°F (180°C). Line a cookie sheet with parchment paper.

**5** In a food processor, combine the dry ingredients. Add the butter and pulse a few times until the mixture resembles coarse sand.

**6** Spread on the cookie sheet. Bake for about 10 minutes. Stir and continue baking until golden brown, about 7 more minutes. Let cool completely.

**7 WHIPPED CREAM**  In a bowl, whip the cream with the maple syrup until soft peaks form. Add the sour cream and whip until combined.

**8 ASSEMBLY**  Spoon the whipped cream over the maple jelly. Spoon the apples over the cream. Top with crumble.

# MAPLE-PECAN BISCOTTI

*Preparation* 15 MINUTES    *Cooking* 50 MINUTES    *Makes* 20 BISCOTTI

1 cup (250 mL) unbleached all-purpose flour
2/3 cup (150 mL) granulated maple sugar
1/2 tsp (2.5 mL) baking powder
1/4 cup (60 mL) cold unsalted butter, cubed
1 egg, lightly beaten
1/2 tsp (2.5 mL) vanilla extract
1/2 cup (125 mL) toasted pecan halves
Milk for brushing

**1** With the rack in the middle position, preheat the oven to 350°F (180°C). Line a cookie sheet with parchment paper.
**2** In a food processor, combine the flour, 1/2 cup (125 mL) maple sugar and the baking powder. Add the butter and pulse until the mixture resembles coarse sand. Add the egg and vanilla. Mix until just combined.
**3** Place the dough in a bowl and continue mixing with your hands, adding the pecans.
**4** On a floured surface, shape the dough into a 12-inch (30 cm) log. Place the log on the baking sheet. Bake for 30 minutes. Transfer to a cutting board.
**5** Let cool for about 15 minutes. Brush with milk and dust with the remaining maple sugar.
**6** Using a very sharp bread knife, cut diagonally into 3/4-inch (2 cm) slices.
**7** Arrange the slices on the baking sheet and return to the oven for about 20 minutes. Let cool on a rack.

It's always a good idea to impress your boss. But you can't be seen *trying* to impress. If the effort is too obvious, you'll look like you're engaging in blatant flattery. Fail, and you'll come across as incompetent. So how do you pull it off? With a torrent of champagne and a mountain of caviar? I don't know your boss, but mine has more money than me. A lot more. He can have champagne and caviar for breakfast every day. How about serving sculpted food worthy of a Dubai architect? He'll only wonder where you found the time to cook such masterpieces and conclude that you did it on his dime. To impress the boss at home, you need to do what you do at the office: do things he can't do. True, when it comes to some bosses that leaves the field pretty much wide open. At work, you don't try to impress the boss by imitating him. You approach your projects from a new perspective. Likewise, your dinner won't impress anyone if you simply try to copy the great chefs. No, what you have to do is choose high-quality, attractive products, present them carefully but simply, and look for a new angle. No doubt about it: simplicity is always a winning strategy.

honey, I invited THE BOSS → FOR DINNER

# attractive and tasteful

# LICHEE MARTINI

*Preparation* 10 MINUTES          *Serves* 6

**If you can't find lichee juice, use the syrup from canned lichees.**

6 fresh lichees, peeled and pitted or canned lichees
1 cup (250 mL) lichee juice
1/2 cup (125 mL) pink grapefruit juice, preferably freshly squeezed
1/2 cup (125 mL) chilled vodka
Ice cubes
6 thin slices lime

**1** Freeze the lichees. In a cocktail shaker or small pitcher, combine the lichee juice, grapefruit juice, vodka and ice cubes. Shake or stir well. Strain into martini glasses. Garnish each drink with 1 lichee and 1 lime slice.

# CREAM OF SHALLOT SOUP

*Preparation* 10 MINUTES          *Cooking* 30 MINUTES          *Serves* 4 TO 6

3/4 lb (350 g) shallots, peeled and quartered (2 cups/500 mL)
2 Tbsp (30 mL) butter
4 cups (1 L) chicken broth
1/2 cup (125 mL) heavy cream (35%)
3 egg yolks
Salt and pepper

**1** In a saucepan over medium heat, soften the shallots in the butter. Add the broth and bring to a boil. Cover, reduce the heat and simmer gently until the shallots are tender, about 20 minutes.
**2** Purée in a blender until smooth. Return the soup to the saucepan.
**3** In a bowl, whisk together the cream and egg yolks. Pour the mixture into the soup in a thin stream, stirring constantly.
**4** Reheat the soup over low heat while stirring with a wooden spoon. Do not allow to boil. Cook until slightly thickened. Season with salt and pepper. If making in advance, do not boil when reheating.

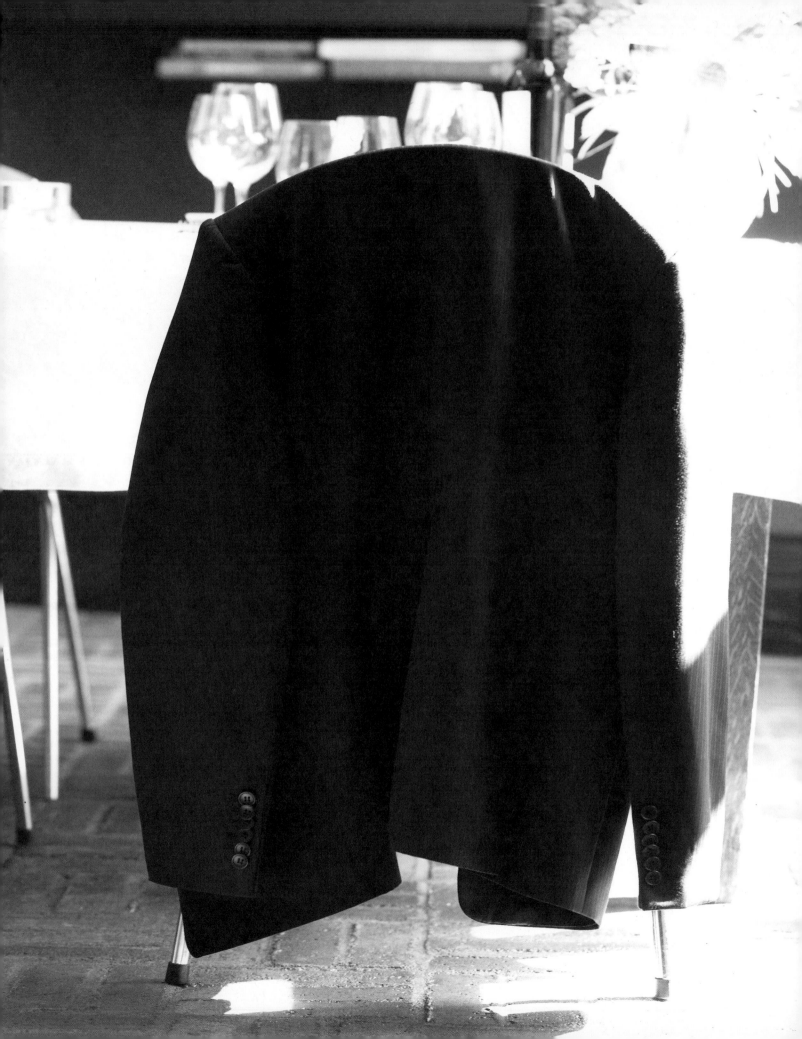

# OYSTERS WITH PINK GRAPEFRUIT

*Preparation* 30 MINUTES      *Makes* 12 OYSTERS

1 pink grapefruit
2 Tbsp (30 mL) rice vinegar
2 tsp (10 mL) chopped fresh chives
Grated zest of 1 lemon
1 Tbsp (15 mL) lemon juice
1 tsp (5 mL) sugar
12 fresh oysters, scrubbed
Crushed ice or coarse sea salt

**1** Section the grapefruit. To do this, slice off the ends. Stand the grapefruit on a cutting board. Using a very sharp knife, slice off the peel and white membrane, exposing the flesh. Holding the fruit in your hand, slide the blade between each section and lift out the flesh. Work over a bowl to collect any juice.

**2** Chop the sections into small pieces. Place in a bowl. Squeeze any juice out of the remaining grapefruit over the bowl. Add all remaining ingredients except the oysters. Refrigrate while preparing the oysters.

**3** Shuck the oysters and detach the flesh from the shells. Place the half-shells on a serving plate covered with crushed ice or coarse salt. Spoon the grapefruit mixture over the oysters. Serve immediately.

# SMOKED TROUT RILLETTES

*Preparation* 5 MINUTES        *Cooking* 10 MINUTES        *Refrigeration* 3 HOURS        *Serves* 6

3/4 cup (180 mL) heavy cream (35%)
1 shallot, thinly sliced
2 sprigs fresh thyme
1/2 tsp (2.5 mL) cracked black peppercorns
2 Tbsp (30 mL) unsalted butter
5 oz (150 g) sliced smoked trout
2 egg yolks
1 Tbsp (15 mL) brandy

**1** In a saucepan, bring the cream, shallot, thyme, pepper and butter to a boil. Reduce by half over medium heat. Pour the cream through a sieve and return it to the saucepan. Add the trout and continue cooking over medium heat for 3 minutes while stirring.

**2** In a bowl, mix the egg yolks and the brandy. Whisk in a small amount of the hot cream to temper the mixture. Pour this mixture into the saucepan and bring to a boil while whisking.

**3** Pour the rillettes into two 1/2-cup (125 mL) ramekins and cover with plastic wrap. Refrigerate for 3 hours. Serve with toasted baguette slices and assorted pickles (gherkins, pickled onions). Rillettes are best served at around room temperature.

# FOIE GRAS AU TORCHON

*Preparation* 15 MINUTES       *Refrigeration* 48 HOURS       *Cooking* 25 MINUTES       *Serves* 8 TO 10

1 whole duck foie gras, about 1 lb (500 g)
1 cup (250 mL) ice cider or icewine
Chicken broth to cover the foie gras

**1** Let the foie gras stand at room temperature for about 1 hour.
**2** Devein the foie gras: Gently pull apart the 2 lobes. Make a shallow incision in the smaller lobe at the point where it was attached to the larger lobe. Using tweezers or the tip of a thin-bladed knife, carefully pull out all visible veins.
**3** Sprinkle both sides of the foie gras with salt and pepper. Place in a glass dish. Add the ice cider. Cover and refrigerate for 24 hours.
**4** Remove the dish from the refrigerator and let stand at room temperature for 30 minutes. Drain, reserving the marinade.
**5** Wrap the foie gras in a clean tea towel or piece of cheesecloth. Shape it into a cylinder 3 inches (7.5 cm) in diameter, then wrap the tea towel in a long sheet of plastic wrap. Seal tightly by twisting and tying both ends.
**6** In a saucepan, combine the marinade and enough broth to cover the foie gras. Clip a thermometer to the side of the saucepan and heat until the temperature reaches 140°F (60°C). Place the wrapped foie gras in the liquid and poach for 25 minutes, maintaining the temperature at 140°F (60°C).
**7** Remove the foie gras and refrigerate for 24 hours.
**8** Carefully unwrap the foie gras. Slice and serve with slices of toasted brioche and *fleur de sel*, or use a portion for the Roast Chicken with Foie Gras (page 173).

# SCALLOP TARTARE

*Preparation* 15 MINUTES  *Refrigeration* 30 MINUTES  *Makes* 12 HORS D'OEUVRES

Caviar is certainly impressive, but how many people truly appreciate fish eggs? Did you know that some good stuff comes from Quebec's Abitibi region, near Ontario? It's sturgeon roe—the only fish egg that can officially be called caviar—and it's absolutely delicious. Just in case there's someone squeamish around, it's only a garnish in this dish. That way, everyone will be eased into the discovery of its fabulous flavour.

1/2 lb (225 g) very fresh scallops, chopped with a knife
2 Tbsp (30 mL) dried cranberries, finely chopped
2 Tbsp (30 mL) finely chopped fresh chives
2 Tbsp (30 mL) grapefruit juice
1 Tbsp (15 mL) olive oil
Caviar or other fish roe for garnishing
Salt and pepper

**1** In a bowl, combine all ingredients except the caviar. Season with salt and pepper. Refrigerate for about 30 minutes.
**2** Divide the tartare among 12 Chinese soup spoons. Garnish with caviar.

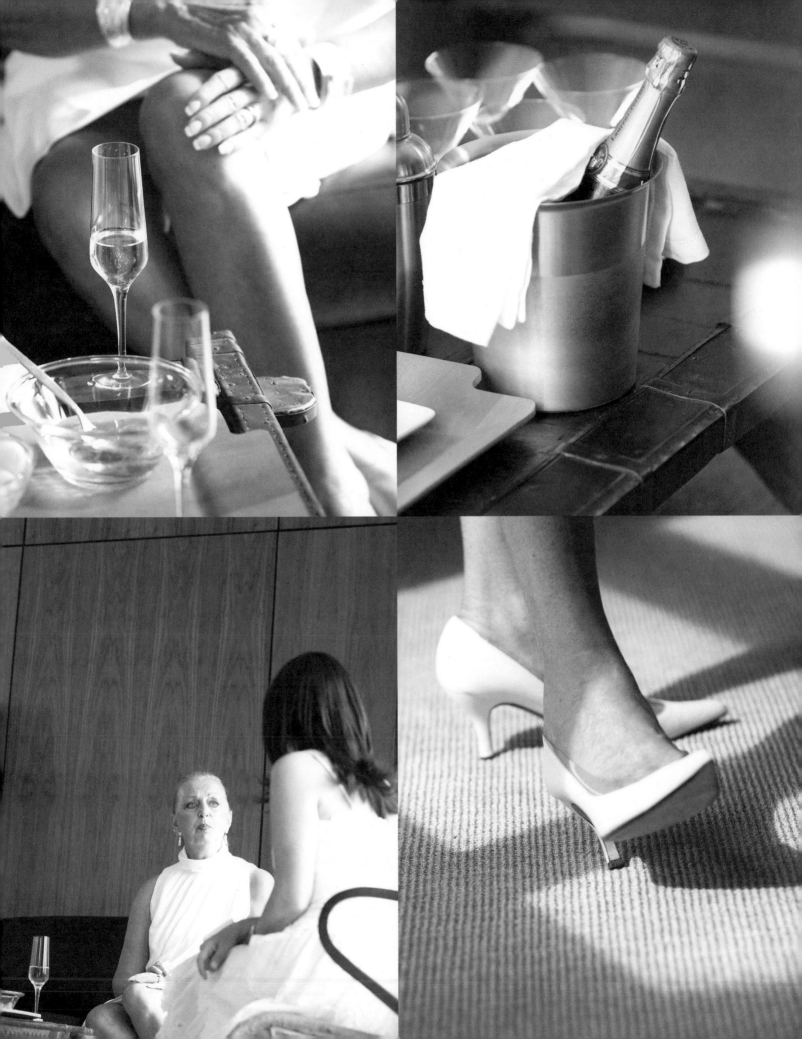

# BEEF "CAPPUCCINO" WITH PARSNIP FOAM

*Preparation* 20 MINUTES    *Cooking* 1 HOUR 30 MINUTES    *Refrigeration* 45 MINUTES
*Serves* 6 TO 8

**A dish's name is a big part of what makes it impressive. So, a simple beef broth is one thing, but quite another when it's a "cappuccino." Likewise, call carrot soup by its glamour name, Crécy, and top it off with an elegant garnish.**

*Parsnip foam*
2 cups (500 mL) peeled, diced parsnips
1 Tbsp (15 mL) butter
2/3 cup (150 mL) milk
2/3 cup (150 mL) heavy cream (35%), whipped

*Beef bouillon*
3 lb (1.5 kg) beef soup bones
3 carrots, cut in thick rounds
3 stalks celery, cut in large pieces
2 cloves garlic, peeled
1 onion, quartered
2 Tbsp (30 mL) olive oil
6 cups (1.5 L) water
Salt and pepper

**1 PARSNIP FOAM** Place the parsnips in a saucepan and add water to cover. Add salt and bring to a boil. Boil until tender. Drain.
**2** In a food processor, purée the parsnips with the butter. Add the milk in a thin stream and process until smooth. Refrigerate until well chilled, about 45 minutes.
**3** In a bowl, gently combine the parsnip purée and the whipped cream. Refrigerate.
**4 BEEF BOUILLON** With the rack in the middle position, preheat the oven to 500°F (260°C).
**5** On a rimmed baking sheet, combine all ingredients except the water. Sprinkle with salt. Roast until the bones are well browned, 35 to 45 minutes, turning 3 times during cooking. Remove from the oven and transfer to a saucepan. Add the water and bring to a boil. Reduce the heat and simmer for 40 to 45 minutes. Strain and degrease.
**6** Heat the parsnip foam in a microwave oven for about 2 minutes. Pour hot broth into espresso or cappuccino cups and top with dollops of parsnip foam. Season with freshly ground pepper. Serve with a small spoon.

RECIPE P167

# SKATE WITH WATERCRESS SAUCE

*Preparation* 15 MINUTES          *Cooking* 20 MINUTES          *Serves* 4 (MAIN COURSE) OR 8 (APPETIZER)

3 lb (1.5 kg) skate wing, skin removed from both sides, cut in 4 or 8 pieces, rinsed and patted dry
2 Tbsp (30 mL) olive oil
2 Tbsp (30 mL) butter
Salt and pepper

*Watercress sauce*
1 small onion, finely chopped
2 cloves garlic, finely chopped
2 Tbsp (30 mL) olive oil
4 cups (1 L) watercress
1/4 cup (60 mL) chicken broth
1/2 cup (125 mL) heavy cream (35%)

**1** With the rack in the middle position, preheat the oven to 350°F (180°C). Line a baking sheet with parchment paper.
**2** In a large non-stick skillet over medium heat, lightly brown the skate wings on both sides, 2 pieces at a time, in half the oil and butter. Season with salt and pepper. Transfer to the baking sheet. Bake until the meat pulls easily from the cartilage, about 20 minutes.
**3 WATERCRESS SAUCE**  Meanwhile, in the same skillet over medium heat, soften the onion and garlic in the oil. Add the watercress and cook for about 2 minutes. Add the broth and cream and continue cooking for about 2 minutes. Season with salt and pepper.
**4** In a blender, purée the sauce until smooth. Adjust the seasoning. Serve as a main course or as an appetizer.

# ROASTED DUCK MAGRET WITH SPICED WHISKY SAUCE

*Preparation* 30 MINUTES     *Cooking* 30 MINUTES     *Serves* 4

When you're looking for a touch of class, few foods do the job better than duck. What's the difference between the breast and the magret? Both come from the same part of the bird, but the magret is from ducks that were fattened for foie gras, so it's usually larger. It also requires last-minute cooking, so you probably shouldn't attempt it if you're serving more than six people. For larger dinner parties, check out our ideas for stews and casseroles in the chapter called "They're always late." If you like beef, you will enjoy duck magret.

*Sauce*
2 shallots, finely chopped
1/4 cup (60 mL) honey
1/4 cup (60 mL) whisky or Scotch
2 cups (500 mL) chicken broth
4 to 6 star anise pods (to taste)
1 tsp (5 mL) crushed pepper
1 clove
Salt

*Duck*
2 duck magrets, about 1 lb (500 g) each or 4 breasts
3 cloves garlic, peeled
3 sprigs fresh thyme
Salt and pepper

**1 SAUCE** In a small saucepan, sauté the shallot and honey until the honey begins to caramelize. Deglaze with the whisky. If desired, flambé to burn off the alcohol. Add the remaining ingredients. Bring to a boil and reduce by half. Season with salt. Set aside.

**2 DUCK** With the rack in the middle position, preheat the oven to 350°F (180°C). Using a sharp knife, score the skin of magrets in a large crosshatch pattern, without cutting into the meat. Season with salt and pepper.

**3** In an ovenproof skillet over medium heat, brown the magrets skin side down with the garlic and thyme until the skin is crisp, 12 to 15 minutes. Remove the rendered fat and set aside. Turn the magrets and continue cooking over medium heat for about 2 minutes. Transfer to the oven and roast for 5 to 7 minutes for medium rare. Place the breasts on a plate, tent with foil and let rest for about 5 minutes. Remove any fat from the skillet and deglaze with the sauce.

**4** Slice the magrets. Serve with Classic Mashed Potatoes (page 171) and your choice of vegetables (for example, Miniature Vegetables Roasted in Olive Oil, page 170). Drizzle with the sauce.

# MINIATURE VEGETABLES ROASTED IN OLIVE OIL

*Preparation* 10 MINUTES     *Cooking* 45 MINUTES     *Serves* 4

**If you can't get your hands on miniature vegetables, substitute larger but still elegant-looking vegetables, such as asparagus, or carrots with a small amount of stem attached.**

8 pearl onions or cipollini, peeled
8 miniature bell peppers in assorted colours
8 miniature squashes in assorted colours
4 miniature eggplants, halved
4 miniature zucchini
2 Tbsp (30 mL) olive oil
1 sprig fresh rosemary
1 sprig fresh thyme
1 Tbsp (15 mL) finely chopped fresh chives
Salt and pepper

**1** With the rack in the middle position, preheat the oven to 350°F (180°C).
**2** In a 9- x 13-inch (23 x 33 cm) baking dish, combine all the ingredients except the chives. Season with salt and pepper. Roast until the vegetables are tender, about 45 minutes. Sprinkle with chives.
**3** Serve with duck, other poultry or beef.

# CLASSIC MASHED POTATOES

*Preparation* 15 MINUTES     *Cooking* 15 MINUTES     *Serves* 6

6 cups (1.5 L) Yukon gold potatoes, peeled and cut in pieces (about 8 potatoes)
4 cloves garlic, peeled
1/4 cup (60 mL) butter
1/2 cup (125 mL) milk (approx)
Salt and pepper

**1** In a large saucepan of salted water over medium-high heat, boil the potatoes and garlic until tender, about 15 minutes. Drain.
**2** Mash the potatoes and garlic with the butter. Add the milk and purée using an electric mixer. Season with salt and pepper. For a variation, substitute buttermilk for the milk and add chopped fresh chives.

# ROAST CHICKEN WITH FOIE GRAS

*Preparation* 25 MINUTES   *Refrigeration* 2 HOURS   *Cooking* 1 HOUR 35 MINUTES
*Serves* 4 TO 6

### Stuffed chicken
1/2 cup (125 mL) duck fat or softened butter
1/4 lb (115 g) Foie Gras au Torchon (page 159 or store-bought), at room temperature
1 chicken, about 4 lb (1.8 kg)
1 Tbsp (15 mL) breadcrumbs
Salt and pepper

### Sauce (optional)
1/2 cup (125 mL) chicken broth
1/4 cup (60 mL) icewine or Sauternes
2 Tbsp (30 mL) flour

**1** Line a baking sheet with parchment paper.

**2 STUFFED CHICKEN** Set aside 1 Tbsp (15 mL) of duck fat. In a food processor, mix the foie gras with the rest of the duck fat.

**3** Butterfly the chicken: Place the chicken on its back on a cutting board and use a chef's knife to cut through the back along one side of the backbone.

**4** Work your fingers under the skin of the breast and thighs, separating it from the meat. Take care to avoid tearing the skin. Spread the foie gras mixture evenly under the skin. Lay the chicken flat on the baking sheet. Refrigerate until the foie gras sets, about 2 hours.

**5** With the rack in the middle position, preheat the oven to 375°F (190°C).

**6** Brush the chicken with the reserved duck fat and dust with breadcrumbs. Season with salt and pepper.

**7** Roast until a meat thermometer inserted in the thigh without touching the bone reads 180°F (82°C), 1 hour and 15 minutes to 1-1/2 hours. Keep the chicken warm and reserve the cooking juices and fat for the sauce.

**8 SAUCE** In a saucepan, whisk together the broth, wine and flour until the mixture is smooth. Add the cooking juices and fat and bring to a boil, whisking constantly. Simmer gently for about 2 minutes. Adjust the seasoning.

**9** Serve with Classic Mashed Potatoes (page 171) and carrots.

RECIPE P177

# HONEY-ROASTED FIGS WITH ALMOND PRALINE ICE CREAM

*Preparation* 15 MINUTES     *Cooking* 25 MINUTES     *Freezing* 2 HOURS 15 MINUTES     *Serves* 8

**I first tried this sublime dessert in an Italian restaurant. I was blown away by its simplicity—I never would have thought you could make such a delicious dish with simple roasted figs and a bit of honey. Ever since, I've been dabbling at being Italian, as proven by the fig tree growing in my garden. Every fall, the tree gets moved to my wine cellar for the winter. This year, it yielded about 20 figs.**

### Ice cream
1/2 cup (125 mL) slivered almonds
1/4 cup (60 mL) honey
2 cups (500 mL) firmly frozen vanilla ice cream
2 Tbsp (30 mL) almond butter

### Roasted figs
8 large fresh figs
8 sprigs fresh thyme
1/2 cup (125 mL) honey

**1** Line a baking sheet with parchment paper.

**2 ICE CREAM** In a preheated skillet, cook the almonds and honey over medium heat, stirring constantly until the honey caramelizes and darkens slightly. Pour onto the cookie sheet, spreading the mixture in a thin layer. Transfer the cookie sheet to the freezer until the praline hardens, 15 to 30 minutes. Break the praline into pieces and set aside on parchment paper, including 8 small shards for garnishing.

**3** In a food processor, pulse the ice cream and almond butter until mixed. Add the praline pieces and pulse briefly until the almonds are finely chopped. This step must be done quickly. Transfer to an airtight container. Freeze until firm, about 2 hours.

**4 ROASTED FIGS** With the rack in the middle position, preheat the oven to 350°F (180°C).

**5** Using a knife, cut a cross in the stem end of each fig. Stand the figs in an 8-inch (20 cm) square Pyrex dish. Add the thyme sprigs and drizzle the figs with honey. Roast until the figs swell and partially open like a flower, about 20 minutes. Baste the figs with the cooking juices several times while roasting.

**6** Serve each diner 1 fig and 1 scoop of ice cream. Drizzle with honey and garnish with a praline shard and thyme leaves.

# MUSCAT AND RED GRAPE CAKE

***Preparation*** 20 MINUTES ***Cooking*** 1 HOUR 10 MINUTES ***Serves*** 8

2 cups (500 mL) unbleached all-purpose flour
2 tsp (10 mL) baking powder
1/2 tsp (2.5 mL) salt
1/2 cup (125 mL) unsalted butter, softened
3/4 cup (180 mL) sugar
1/4 cup (60 mL) vegetable oil
Grated zest of 1 orange
1 tsp (5 mL) vanilla extract
2 eggs
1 cup (250 mL) muscat wine (Muscat de Beaumes de Venise)
2 cups (500 mL) red seedless grapes
2 Tbsp (30 mL) honey

**1** With the rack in the middle position, preheat the oven to 350°F (180°C). Line an 8-inch (20 cm) springform pan with parchment paper. Butter the pan.
**2** In a bowl, combine the flour, baking powder and salt. Set aside.
**3** In another bowl, cream the butter with the sugar, oil, orange zest and vanilla using an electric mixer. Add the eggs one at a time, beating until smooth. With the mixer on low speed, add the dry ingredients, alternating with the wine.
**4** Using a spatula, fold half the grapes into the batter.
**5** Scrape the batter into the pan. Arrange the remaining grapes on top, pressing them lightly into the batter, and drizzle the honey on top. Bake until a toothpick inserted in the centre comes out clean, about 1 hour and 10 minutes.
**6** Let cool slightly. Unmould and finish cooling on a cake rack.

# ICED MAPLE-PECAN PRALINE PARFAIT

***Preparation*** 40 MINUTES    ***Cooking*** 20 MINUTES    ***Refrigeration*** 30 MINUTES
***Freezing*** 6 HOURS    ***Serves*** 8

### Maple caramel
1/2 cup (125 mL) maple syrup
1 Tbsp (15 mL) corn syrup
1/4 cup (60 mL) heavy cream (35%), hot

### Pecan pralines
3 Tbsp (45 mL) maple syrup
1 Tbsp (15 mL) corn syrup
1/2 cup (125 mL) pecan halves, toasted

### Ice cream
1-1/2 cups (375 mL) heavy cream (35%)
1/4 cup (60 mL) sugar
2 cups (500 mL) vanilla ice cream, softened in the refrigerator for about 15 minutes

**1 MAPLE CARAMEL** In a saucepan, bring the 2 syrups to a boil. Simmer, without stirring, until a candy thermometer reads 270°F (132°C). Remove from the heat and slowly add the cream. Take care to avoid spatters. Bring to a boil, stirring constantly until the mixture is smooth. Remove from the heat and pour into a large bowl. (A larger bowl helps the caramel cool faster.) Freeze, stirring frequently, until the caramel reaches room temperature, 15 to 20 minutes.
**2** Line a lightly oiled 8-inch (20 cm) square Pyrex baking dish with plastic wrap. Line a cookie sheet with parchment paper.
**3 PECAN PRALINES** In a small saucepan, bring the 2 syrups to a boil. Simmer, without stirring, until the syrup starts to caramelize, about 1 minute. Add the pecans and stir to coat well. Spread on the cookie sheet. Let cool. Chop and set aside.
**4 ICE CREAM** In a bowl, beat the cream and sugar with an electric mixer until stiff peaks form. With the mixer on low speed, add the ice cream and mix until smooth. Fold in the pecans. Spread half the mixture in the baking dish. Pour half the caramel over it in a spiral pattern. Gently spread the remaining ice cream mixture on top. Pour the remaining caramel on top in a spiral. Run a knife through the parfait to create a marbled effect. Freeze for 6 hours or overnight.
**5** Let stand at room temperature for 5 minutes before serving. Unmould and cut into squares or slices.

RECIPE P178

# WHITE CHOCOLATE POTS DE CRÈME WITH PASSIONFRUIT JELLY

*Preparation* 25 MINUTES    *Cooking* 15 MINUTES    *Refrigeration* 6 HOURS    *Serves* 6

### Pots de crème
1 tsp (5 mL) gelatin
3 Tbsp (45 mL) water
8 oz (250 g) white chocolate, finely chopped
1/4 cup (60 mL) unsalted butter
3 eggs, lightly beaten
1/2 cup (125 mL) heavy cream (35%), hot
1/4 cup (60 mL) milk, hot

### Passionfruit jelly
1 tsp (5 mL) gelatin
1-1/4 cups (310 mL) passionfruit juice
1 Tbsp (15 mL) sugar

### Topping
1/2 cup (125 mL) fresh strawberries, finely diced
1 Tbsp (15 mL) sugar
1/4 tsp (1 mL) Szechuan peppercorns, crushed

**1 POTS DE CRÈME**  Pour the water in a bowl and sprinkle the gelatin onto it. Let soften for 5 minutes.

**2** Melt the chocolate and butter in the top part of a double boiler. Remove from the heat and whisk in the eggs. Add the cream and milk. Return to the heat. Whisking constantly and taking care to scrape the bottom and corners of the pan, continue cooking until slightly thickened. Add the gelatin and stir until dissolved.

**3** Pour the mixture into 6 flared-rim cups or cocktail glasses. Refrigerate for about 3 hours.

**4 PASSIONFRUIT JELLY**  In a small saucepan, sprinkle the gelatin onto 1/2 cup (125 mL) of the juice. Let soften for about 5 minutes. Add the sugar and heat gently, stirring constantly, until the gelatin and sugar dissolve. Add the remaining juice and stir to combine. Let cool partially.

**5** Pour carefully onto the pots de crème. Refrigerate for about 3 hours.

**6 TOPPING**  Just before serving, place the strawberries in a bowl and toss with the remaining sugar and the Szechuan pepper. Let stand for about 5 minutes. Pile the strawberries on each pot de crème.

# BEET CAKES WITH MASCARPONE CREAM

*Preparation* 35 MINUTES       *Cooking* 35 MINUTES       *Serves* 12

## Cakes
1 cup (250 mL) peeled and grated beets
1/2 cup (125 mL) unsalted butter
1 Tbsp (15 mL) lemon juice
1 cup (250 mL) unbleached all-purpose flour
1 tsp (5 mL) baking powder
1/4 tsp (1 mL) salt
2 eggs
1 cup (250 mL) sugar
Grated zest of 1 lemon
1 tsp (5 mL) vanilla extract
1/2 cup (125 mL) slivered almonds

## Beet syrup
1/2 cup (125 mL) water
1/2 cup (125 mL) honey
1/2 cup (125 mL) sugar
1/2 cup (125 mL) peeled, grated beets

## Mascarpone cream
1/2 lb (250 g) container mascarpone cheese
1/2 cup (125 mL) heavy cream (35%)
2 Tbsp (30 mL) sugar
Grated zest of 1 lemon

**1 CAKES**  With the rack in the middle position, preheat the oven to 350°F (180°C). Butter and flour 12 muffin cups.

**2** In a saucepan over medium heat, soften the beets in the butter and lemon juice, about 5 minutes. Let cool partially. Refrigerate until the beets reach room temperature.

**3** In a bowl, combine the flour, baking powder and salt.

**4** In another bowl, beat the eggs, sugar, lemon zest and vanilla using an electric mixer, about 2 minutes. With the mixer on low speed, add the dry ingredients, alternating with the beet mixture.

**5** Divide the batter among the muffin cups. Sprinkle with almonds. Bake until a toothpick inserted in the centre of a cake comes out clean.

**6** Loosen the cakes by running a knife around the inside of each muffin cup. Unmould carefully, without inverting, and place on a cooling rack. Let cool completely.

**7 BEET SYRUP**  In a small saucepan, bring all the ingredients to a boil, stirring constantly. Reduce the heat and simmer until slightly syrupy, about 10 minutes. Strain. Discard the beets. Let cool partially and refrigerate until chilled.

**8 MASCARPONE CREAM**  In a bowl, whip all the ingredients using an electric mixer until stiff peaks form.

**9** Spread about 3 Tbsp (45 mL) mascarpone cream on each plate. Place a cake in the centre. Drizzle with a thin stream of beet syrup.

Latecomers have always been the bane of humanity. They might just be the worst thing ever, next to badly translated instruction manuals. The chronically tardy stop planes from taking off on time, they thwart our attempts to rent that new release from the video store, and they embarrass us when they leave us sitting alone, trying to hold a seat for them in a restaurant. Not to mention all the overdone roasts, desiccated chickens and flat champagne they're responsible for. Of course, there are ways to get revenge. You could come to the door in your pyjamas, toothbrush poking out of your mouth, and say: "Oh, there you are!" A flannel robe and curlers will really drive your point home. Especially if you're a man. Or you can plan around the chronically late by making soups and stews that you can serve whenever. I have a few friends who think I only know how to cook stews! They're in for a surprise if they ever show up on time!

tHeY're ALWAYS LATE

# stews and other dishes that can wait

RARE

MEDIUM

TRASH

WELL DONE

CHARRED

VERY WELL DONE

RECIPE P194

# CREAM OF BRIE SOUP

*Preparation* 15 MINUTES     *Cooking* 20 MINUTES     *Serves* 4 TO 6

3 shallots, chopped
2 Tbsp (30 mL) butter
2 Tbsp (30 mL) unbleached all-purpose flour
1/2 cup (125 mL) white wine
2 cups (500 mL) milk
1 cup (250 mL) chicken broth
3/4 lb (350 g) brie, trimmed of rind and cubed
Salt and pepper

**1** In a saucepan, lightly sauté the shallots in the butter for about 10 minutes. Dust with flour and cook for about 1 minute, stirring constantly. Deglaze with the wine and stir. Add the milk and broth. Bring to a boil, reduce the heat and simmer for 5 minutes. Remove from the heat and add the brie. Let melt, about 1 minute.
**2** In a blender, purée the soup until smooth. Adjust the seasoning. Reheat on low.
**3** Serve in small bowls and garnish with Mushroom Duxelles.

# MUSHROOM DUXELLES

*Preparation* 10 MINUTES     *Cooking* 15 MINUTES     *Makes* 3/4 CUP (180 ML)

1/2 lb (225 g) white mushrooms, finely chopped
1 shallot, finely chopped
2 Tbsp (30 mL) butter
1/2 cup (125 mL) white wine
2 Tbsp (30 mL) finely chopped fresh chives
Salt and pepper

**1** In a skillet over medium heat, sauté the mushrooms and shallot in the butter until golden brown. Season with salt and pepper. Deglaze with the wine. Bring to a boil and reduce until nearly dry. Add the chives.
**2** Use as a garnish for the Cream of Brie Soup.

# CHOISY SOUP

***Preparation*** 15 MINUTES  ***Cooking*** 25 MINUTES  ***Serves*** 6

**You can make this soup with leftover lettuce. It's just as good cold as it is hot. Feel that? That's your stress level dropping.**

1 onion, chopped
2 Tbsp (30 mL) butter
3 cups (750 mL) chicken broth
3 cups (750 mL) peeled and cubed potatoes
2 cups (500 mL) milk
6 cups (1.5 L) coarsely chopped lettuce
Salt and pepper
1/3 cup (75 mL) sour cream
18 cherry tomatoes, quartered

**1** In a saucepan over medium heat, soften the onions in the butter. Add the broth, potatoes and milk. Season with salt and pepper. Bring to a boil. Reduce the heat, cover and simmer gently until the potatoes are tender, about 20 minutes.
**2** Add the lettuce. Bring to a boil and cook for 1 or 2 minutes. Purée the soup in a blender. Adjust the seasoning. Serve hot or cold.
**3** To serve, garnish with sour cream and cherry tomatoes.

# CABBAGE AND BEET SOUP

***Preparation*** 20 MINUTES  ***Cooking*** 30 MINUTES  ***Serves*** 4 TO 6

1 onion, chopped
2 Tbsp (30 mL) olive oil
1 Tbsp (15 mL) brown sugar
2 Tbsp (30 mL) white wine vinegar
6 cups (1.5 L) chicken broth
2 medium potatoes, peeled and diced
2 medium beets, peeled and julienned (2 cups/500 mL)
2 cups (500 mL) finely sliced green cabbage
1/4 cup (60 mL) flat-leaf parsley, chopped
Salt and pepper

**1** In a saucepan, brown the onion in the oil. Add the brown sugar and cook, stirring constantly, for 1 minute. Deglaze with the vinegar. Add the remaining ingredients except the parsley. Season with salt and pepper. Bring to a boil. Cover, reduce the heat and simmer until the vegetables are tender, about 25 minutes. Add the parsley and adjust the seasoning.

can
wait
24 HRS Fridge

# LEEKS AND CELERY VINAIGRETTE

*Preparation* 15 MINUTES          *Cooking* 20 MINUTES          *Serves* 6

**Here's a main course that you can serve lukewarm or even cold, so there's no need to worry if you're sitting down to dinner on the late side. While you're waiting for your guests, let it sit at room temperature but keep the vinaigrette in the fridge; all you have to do is add it at the last minute. The things we do for the ones we love.**

6 medium or small leeks
3 stalks celery, cut in 2 lengths
1-1/4 cups (310 mL) chicken broth
1 sprig fresh thyme
1 bay leaf
1 clove
1/3 cup (75 mL) cider vinegar
1 egg yolk
1-1/2 tsp (7.5 mL) Dijon mustard
1/3 cup (75 mL) olive oil
Salt and pepper
1 green apple, halved, cored and thinly sliced on a mandoline

**1** With the rack in the middle position, preheat the oven to 350°F (180°C).
**2** Remove the dark green portion of the leeks and discard. Cut the light green and white parts in half crosswise.
**3** Arrange the leek and celery sections in a baking dish. Add the broth, thyme, bay leaf and clove. Season with salt and pepper. Cover with foil. Bake for about 30 minutes. Remove the leeks and celery and set aside to cool. Strain the broth.
**4** Pour 1/3 cup (75 mL) of the broth into a saucepan with the vinegar. Reduce until 3 Tbsp (45 mL) of liquid remain. Let cool.
**5** In a bowl, whisk together the vinegar reduction, egg yolk and mustard. Add the oil in a thin stream, whisking constantly. Season with salt and pepper. Transfer the vegetables and apples to plates and dress with the vinaigrette.

RECIPE P201

# CABBAGE STUFFED WITH THREE CHEESES

*Preparation* 45 MINUTES  *Cooking* 1 HOUR 45 MINUTES  *Resting* 15 MINUTES
*Serves* 6 TO 8

**I came up with this recipe for the day after dinner parties, when there's usually a pile of cheese scraps to be used up. Not only is it original, but you can keep it in a warm oven for a long time.**

10 Savoy cabbage leaves
1-1/2 cups (375 mL) finely sliced leeks
2 Tbsp (30 mL) butter, softened
1/4 cup (60 mL) white wine
1/4 lb (115 g) Riopelle cheese or other triple cream brie, rind removed
1/4 lb (115 g) Oka, Iberville or other washed-rind cheese, rind removed, cubed
6 russet potatoes, peeled and cut in 1/8-inch (3 mm) slices on a mandoline
3 cups (750 mL) milk
1 sprig fresh thyme
1 clove garlic, peeled
1 small butternut squash, top part only, peeled then sliced on a mandoline
1/4 lb (115 g) Valbert cheese or other firm cheese, rind removed, cubed
Salt and pepper

**1** In a large saucepan of boiling salted water, blanch the cabbage leaves until tender, about 4 minutes. Drain and rinse with cold water. Set aside.

**2** In a skillet over medium heat, soften the leeks in the butter. Add the wine and reduce until almost dry. Add the Riopelle and washed-rind cheese. Stir until the cheese melts. Season with salt and pepper. Set aside.

**3** Place the potatoes, milk, thyme and garlic in a saucepan. Season with salt and pepper. Bring to a boil, reduce the heat to medium and simmer until the potatoes are al dente, about 5 minutes. Stir occasionally to prevent the milk from scorching. Remove the thyme and garlic clove. Drain the potatoes and return the milk to the saucepan. Add the squash and bring to a boil. Add milk as needed. Simmer over medium heat until the squash is al dente. Drain and set aside.

**4** With the rack in the middle position, preheat the oven to 375°F (190°C). Line the bottom of a 9-inch (23 cm) springform pan with parchment paper.

**5** Place a large cabbage leaf in the bottom of the pan. Line the sides of the pan with 6 more leaves, letting them hang over the rim. Place another leaf in the bottom. Add two-thirds of the potatoes. Season with salt and pepper. Press down lightly and then add the leek and cheese mixture. Add the rest of the potatoes and the squash. Add a layer of firm cheese and top with a cabbage leaf. Fold the cabbage leaves in toward the centre and cover with a cabbage leaf.

**6** Brush with butter. Wrap the whole pan in 2 sheets of foil. Place it on a cookie sheet. Bake for about 1-1/2 hours. Remove from the oven. Cover the top with a plate. Let stand for 15 minutes.

**7** Unmould and serve with a green salad.

RECIPE P204

# CHICKEN WITH MORELS

*Preparation* 30 MINUTES    *Cooking* 75 MINUTES    *Serves* 4

**It's usually too risky to cook chicken for habitual latecomers. The meat dries out, the flavour drifts away. But when the bird is in a sauce, it's easier to keep things under control. If you dare to do this with a whole chicken, use a meat thermometer. When it reads 180°F (82°C), the chicken is ready. If people are late, stop cooking about 20°F (7°C) before it's done, then resume when they arrive. A handy trick for the savvy cook.**

1-1/2 cups (375 mL) chicken broth
Two 1/2 oz (15 g) packages dried morel mushrooms
1/2 oz (15 g) package dried chanterelle mushrooms
2 tsp (10 mL) cornstarch
2 Tbsp (30 mL) water
1 chicken (4 lb/1.8 kg), cut in 8 pieces, skin removed
2 Tbsp (30 mL) butter
1 onion, chopped
2 cloves garlic, chopped
1/4 cup (60 mL) whisky
1/2 cup (125 mL) heavy cream (35%)
2 tsp (10 mL) Dijon mustard
Salt and pepper

**1** In a small saucepan, bring the broth to a boil. Remove from the heat and add the morels and chanterelles. Let rehydrate for about 30 minutes. Set aside.
**2** In a bowl, dissolve the cornstarch in the water. Add the broth and mushroom mixture. Set aside.
**3** In a large skillet or Dutch oven, brown the chicken in the butter. Season with salt and pepper. Add the onion and garlic and continue cooking for about 2 minutes. Deglaze with the whisky. Add the broth and mushroom mixture, cream and mustard. Bring to a boil while stirring. Cover, reduce the heat and simmer gently for about 45 minutes. Turn the chicken pieces and continue cooking uncovered until the chicken is done, about 15 minutes.
**4** Serve with green beans and Perogies (next page).

# PEROGIES

*Preparation* 40 MINUTES      *Waiting* 30 MINUTES      *Cooking* 15 MINUTES
*Serves* 4 (ABOUT 20 PEROGIES)

**Perogies are Eastern Europe's contribution to the wonderful world of dumplings. Stuff the dough with meat or potatoes, then poach the perogies before pan-searing them. It's a side dish that can accommodate someone who's running "just a few minutes" late.**

### Dough
2 cups (500 mL) unbleached all-purpose flour
1/2 tsp (2.5 mL) salt
6 Tbsp (90 mL) water (approx)
1 egg
1/4 cup (60 mL) olive oil

### Filling
3/4 cup (180 mL) dry mashed potatoes (no milk)
3/4 cup (180 mL) cottage cheese, rinsed and drained
Salt and pepper

### Garnish
2 large shallots, finely sliced
2 Tbsp (30 mL) butter

**1 DOUGH** In a large bowl, combine the flour and salt. Make a well in the centre. Pour the water, egg and 2 Tbsp (30 mL) oil into the well. Mix with a fork or your hands.

**2** Place the dough on a flat surface and knead until smooth. Shape into a disc. Cover with plastic wrap and refrigerate for 30 minutes.

**3 FILLING** In a bowl, combine the potatoes and cottage cheese. Season with salt and pepper. Set aside.

**4** On a floured surface, roll out the dough into a thin sheet. Cut out rounds using a 3-inch (7.5 cm) cutter. Spoon about 2 tsp (10 mL) of the filling onto the centre of each round. Brush the edges of the rounds with water. Fold the rounds over the filling to form half-moons. Press the edges together to seal. Set aside on a floured baking sheet.

**5** Boil the perogies in a large pot of boiling salted water until they float to the surface. Continue cooking for 4 minutes. Drain and coat lightly with oil.

**6** In a skillet, brown the perogies in the remaining oil. Season with salt and pepper. Transfer to a plate and keep warm.

**7 GARNISH** In the same skillet, brown the shallots in the butter. Season with salt and pepper. Spoon over the perogies.

**8** Serve alongside Chicken with Morels (facing page).

RAW
FRIED

RECIPE P205

# BUTTERED SUGAR SNAP PEAS

*Preparation* 5 MINUTES    *Cooking* 5 MINUTES    *Serves* 6

1/2 lb (225 g) sugar snap peas or snow peas, trimmed
2 Tbsp (30 mL) butter
1 Tbsp (15 mL) water

**1** Blanch the sugar snap peas in a saucepan of boiling salted water. Drain.
**2** In a skillet over medium-high heat, sauté the peas in the butter and water for about 2 minutes. Season with salt and pepper.

# 4-HOUR MILK-BRAISED PORK

*Preparation* 20 MINUTES      *Cooking* 4 HOURS      *Serves* 6

One 3 lb (1.5 kg) boneless pork shoulder roast
2 Tbsp (30 mL) butter
4 cups (1 L) milk
2 onions, peeled
1 leek, white part only
4 cloves garlic, peeled
1/4 tsp (1 mL) ground nutmeg
Salt and pepper

**1** With the rack in the middle position, preheat the oven to 350°F (180°C).
**2** In a large ovenproof saucepan, brown the pork roast in the butter. Season with salt and pepper. Add the milk and bring to boil. Add the vegetables and nutmeg. Cover and transfer to the oven for 2-1/2 hours. Don't worry if the milk looks like it's curdling at first; you will be straining the liquid through a sieve.
**3** Uncover and continue cooking until the sauce is reduced by a little less than half, about 1-1/2 hours. Turn the pork over every 20 minutes.
**4** Remove the meat and set aside. Strain the braising liquid. Whisk the sauce and adjust the seasoning.
**5** Serve the pork on a large platter, surrounded by Buttered Sugar Snap Peas (see recipe on facing page). Carve the pork and serve with Mashed Sweet Potatoes (recipe follows).

# MASHED SWEET POTATOES

*Preparation* 10 MINUTES      *Cooking* 1 HOUR 30 MINUTES      *Serves* 6

2 lb (1 kg) sweet potatoes
1/4 cup (60 mL) butter
1/4 cup (60 mL) chicken broth
Salt and pepper

**1** With the rack in the middle position, preheat the oven to 350°F (180°C).
**2** Wrap the sweet potatoes in foil. Bake until tender, about 1-1/2 hours. Peel the sweet potatoes. In a food processor, purée the sweet potatoes with the remaining ingredients. Season with salt and pepper.
**3 QUICK MICROWAVE OVEN METHOD** Prick the sweet potatoes with a fork. Microwave on high for 8 minutes. Turn and cook until tender, another 8 minutes, depending on size. Let cool.

# LAMB SHANKS GLAZED WITH BUCKWHEAT HONEY

*Preparation* 20 MINUTES    *Cooking* 2 HOURS 45 MINUTES    *Serves* 6

6 lamb shanks, about 3/4 lb (350 g) each
2 Tbsp (30 mL) olive oil
2 Tbsp (30 mL) butter
1/4 cup (60 mL) sherry vinegar or red wine vinegar
2 Tbsp (30 mL) brandy
2 cups (500 mL) chicken broth
1/2 cup (125 mL) buckwheat honey
1 orange, sliced
1 onion, peeled and halved
2 cloves garlic, peeled and halved
6 carrots, cut diagonally in 1-inch (2.5 cm) lengths
4 celery stalks, cut diagonally in 1-inch (2.5 cm) lengths
4 parsnips, cut diagonally in 1-inch (2.5 cm) lengths
2 sprigs parsley
Salt and pepper

**1** With the rack in the middle position, preheat the oven to 350°F (180°C).
**2** In a large skillet over medium-high heat, brown the shanks in the oil and butter. Season with salt and pepper. Transfer to a plate and set aside.
**3** Deglaze the pan with the vinegar and brandy. Reduce by half.
**4** Add the broth and honey and bring to a boil. Season with salt and pepper. Return the shanks to the skillet. Add the orange, onion and garlic. Roast for 1 hour, basting the shanks regularly. Place the remaining vegetables around the shanks, making sure they are sitting in the broth. Continue roasting for about 45 minutes or until the meat is nicely glazed. Cover and cook until the vegetables are tender and the meat is falling off the bone, 30 to 45 minutes.
**5** Great with puréed or mashed potatoes.

# PORTUGUESE COD CASSEROLE

*Preparation* 25 MINUTES          *Cooking* 1 HOUR 15 MINUTES          *Serves* 6

**Cod or bacalhau? It's the same fish, but bacalhau (a.k.a. bacalao, baccala) is the salted, dried version, whereas fresh, it's simply cod.**

2 onions, thinly sliced
2 Tbsp (30 mL) olive oil
2 cloves garlic, finely chopped
4 cups (1 L) potatoes, peeled and thinly sliced on a mandoline
3 plum tomatoes, sliced
1/4 cup (60 mL) oil-packed black olives, drained, pitted and finely chopped
2 lb (1 kg) fresh cod fillet
1 cup (250 mL) chicken broth
Salt and pepper

**1** If you're going for maximum authenticity, soak a 12-cup (3 L) terracotta baking dish and its cover in water for about 15 minutes. If using another type of dish, preheat the oven to 400°F (200°C) with the rack in the middle position.

**2** In a skillet, brown the onions in the oil until caramelized. Season with salt and pepper. Add the garlic and continue cooking for 1 minute. Set aside.

**3** Cover the bottom of the baking dish with one-quarter of the potato slices. Add half the tomatoes and olives. Season with salt and pepper. Cover with another quarter of the potatoes. Cover with the onion and garlic mixture. Cover with another quarter of the potatoes, then lay the fish on top. Season with salt and pepper. Cover with the remaining potatoes, tomatoes and olives. Add the broth.

**4** If using a terracotta dish, cover and place in the centre of a cold oven (important). Set the oven to 400°F (200°C). Bake until the potatoes are tender, about 1 hour and 15 minutes (1 hour if using a ceramic or glass dish). Let stand for 15 minutes and serve.

# PROFITEROLES

*Preparation* 35 MINUTES    *Cooking* 1 HOUR    *Waiting* 20 MINUTES
*Makes* 16 PROFITEROLES

**Bake the little balls of choux pastry ahead of time and keep them in the freezer.
To make sure they're nice and crisp, reheat them in a 300°F (150°C) oven for a few
minutes, then let them cool before finishing. Even if it's getting late, it's all good.**

*Choux pastry*
1/2 cup (125 mL) milk
1/2 cup (125 mL) water
1/4 cup (60 mL) unsalted butter
1 tsp (5 mL) sugar
1/4 tsp (1 mL) salt
1 cup (250 mL) unbleached all-purpose flour
4 eggs

*Chocolate sauce*
1/2 cup (125 mL) heavy cream (35%)
3 oz (90 g) semi-sweet chocolate, chopped

Vanilla, pecan or caramel ice cream to taste

**1 CHOUX PASTRY** With the rack in the middle position, preheat the oven to 375°F (190°C). Line a
baking sheet with parchment paper.
**2** In a saucepan, bring the milk, water, butter, sugar and salt to a boil. Remove from the heat. Add the
flour all at once and stir vigorously with a wooden spoon until the dough forms a smooth ball that
pulls away from the sides of the pan.
**3** Return the saucepan to the stove and cook over low heat for about 2 minutes, stirring constantly.
**4** Remove from the heat and let cool for a few minutes. Add the eggs one at a time, beating vigorously
with a wooden spoon after each addition, until the dough is smooth.
**5** Fit a pastry bag with a 1/2-inch (1 cm) plain tip and fill it with the dough. Pipe 16 golf ball–sized balls
onto the baking sheet. Using a moistened finger, smooth out any peaks.
**6** Bake until golden, about 40 minutes. Turn off the oven, open the door partially and let the balls
dry for about 15 minutes. Transfer to a cooling rack and let cool completely.
**7 CHOCOLATE SAUCE** Bring the cream to a boil in a saucepan. Remove from the heat and add the
chocolate. Let stand for 2 minutes. Whisk until the chocolate is melted and the sauce smooth. Keep
warm.
**8** Slice the tops off the pastry balls and fill with scoops of ice cream. Replace the tops. Drizzle with
hot chocolate sauce.

# CHOCOLATE CARROT CAKE

*Preparation* 25 MINUTES    *Cooking* 1 HOUR    *Waiting* 2 HOURS    *Serves* 10 TO 12

### Carrot cake
1-1/2 cups (375 mL) unbleached all-purpose flour
1-1/2 tsp (7.5 mL) baking powder
1/2 tsp (2.5 mL) ground cinnamon
1/4 tsp (1 mL) salt
4 eggs
1-1/2 cups (375 mL) sugar
1 tsp (5 mL) vanilla extract
3/4 cup (180 mL) unsalted butter, melted, at room temperature
2 cups (500 mL) grated carrots
4 oz (110 g) semi-sweet chocolate, coarsely chopped

### Sour cream and white chocolate icing
12 oz (375 g) white chocolate, chopped
1/2 cup (125 mL) sour cream

### Candied carrots
1/2 cup (125 mL) orange juice
1/2 cup (125 mL) sugar
2 small carrots, thinly sliced lengthwise on a mandoline (12 slices needed)

**1 CAKE** With the rack in the middle position, preheat the oven to 350°F (180°C). Butter two 8-inch (20 cm) springform pans. Line the bottoms with parchment paper.

**2** In a bowl, combine the flour, baking powder, cinnamon and salt. Set aside.

**3** In another bowl, beat the eggs, sugar and vanilla using an electric mixer until the mixture turns pale and doubles in volume, about 10 minutes. Using a spatula, gently fold in the melted butter. Gently whisk in the dry ingredients. Add the grated carrots and chocolate.

**4** Pour the batter into the pans. Bake until a toothpick inserted in the centre comes out clean, about 45 minutes. Run a thin knife around the edge of the cake to separate it from the pan. Unmould onto a cooling rack and let cool.

**5 SOUR CREAM AND WHITE CHOCOLATE ICING** Melt the chocolate in the top part of a double boiler. Remove from the heat. Add the sour cream and stir until the mixture is smooth. Set aside until the cake is fully cooled, about 2 hours.

**6** Using an electric mixer, beat the chocolate mixture until it stiffens slightly, about 2 minutes. If necessary, refrigerate for a few minutes. Ice the top of both cakes. Set one cake on top of the other.

**7 CANDIED CARROTS** In a saucepan, bring the orange juice and sugar to a boil. Add the sliced carrots. Simmer until tender and translucent, about 8 minutes depending on thickness. Let cool completely. Drain. Arrange rolled carrot strips on the cake to mark the slices.

# MASCARPONE-FREE TIRAMISÙ

*Preparation* 25 MINUTES      *Refrigeration* 2 HOURS      *Serves* 8

1 cup (250 mL) hot espresso or strong coffee
3/4 cup (180 mL) sugar
16 oz (500 g) ricotta
1/2 cup (125 mL) light cream cheese, at room temperature
2 Tbsp (30 mL) coffee or chocolate liqueur
3 egg whites
12 to 14 ladyfingers
1 Tbsp (15 mL) cocoa powder

**1** In a bowl, dissolve 2 Tbsp (30 mL) sugar in the coffee. Refrigerate.

**2** In a food processor, mix the ricotta, cream cheese and liqueur until very smooth. Set aside.

**3** In a large bowl, beat the egg whites until soft peaks form. Gradually add the remaining sugar, beating until stiff peaks form. Using a spatula, gently fold the cheese mixture into the egg whites.

**4** Dip the ladyfingers in the coffee to soak quickly. Line the bottom of a 12-cup (3 L) glass serving bowl with half the ladyfingers. Cover with half of the cheese mixture. Lay the remaining ladyfingers on the cheese mixture. Top with the remaining cheese mixture. Using a fine-mesh sieve, dust the top with cocoa powder. Refrigerate for at least 2 hours before serving.

# PORTUGUESE FLAN

*Preparation* 20 MINUTES     *Cooking* 1 HOUR 15 MINUTES     *Refrigeration* 3 HOURS
*Serves* 10

### Caramel
1/2 cup (125 mL) sugar
2 Tbsp (30 mL) water

### Flan
3/4 cup (180 mL) sugar
2 Tbsp (30 mL) water
2 cups (500 mL) heavy cream (35%), hot
1-1/4 cups (310 mL) milk, hot
6 eggs
2 egg yolks

**1** With the rack in the middle position, preheat the oven to 300°F (150°C).

**2 CARAMEL** In a saucepan, bring the sugar and water to a boil. Simmer, without stirring, until it turns golden. Remove from the heat. Using a silicone brush, paint the interior of a 6-cup (1.5 L) Bundt pan, 3-1/2 inches (8 cm) tall, with the caramel. Work quickly, before the caramel can harden.

**3 FLAN** In a saucepan, bring 1/2 cup (125 mL) sugar and the water to a boil. Simmer until the mixture turns golden. Remove from the heat and slowly add the cream. Take care to avoid spatters. Bring to a boil, without stirring, and cook until smooth. Add the milk and mix well. Set aside.

**4** In a bowl, whisk together the eggs, egg yolks and remaining sugar. Whisk in the hot milk mixture. Strain. Pour the mixture into the Bundt pan. Prepare a *bain-marie*: Line a large roasting pan with a tea towel. Place the Bundt pan in the roasting pan and add enough boiling water to reach halfway up the sides of the Bundt pan. Bake until just set, about 1 hour and 15 minutes. Remove the Bundt pan from the *bain-marie*. Let cool. Refrigerate until fully cooled, about 3 hours. Place the pan in a bath of boiling water for a few seconds. Unmould onto a serving plate.

# TRIFLE WITH PEARS AND CARAMEL

*Preparation* 35 MINUTES     *Cooking* 20 MINUTES     *Refrigeration* 4 HOURS
*Serves* 8 TO 10

**It's even better the next day—the perfect dessert if you expect to be kept waiting.**

*Pastry cream*
1 cup (250 mL) milk
1/2 cup (125 mL) heavy cream (35%)
1/4 cup (60 mL) sugar
3 Tbsp (45 mL) unbleached all-purpose flour
6 egg yolks
1 tsp (5 mL) vanilla extract

*Caramelized pears*
2 Tbsp (30 mL) water
1/4 cup (60 mL) sugar
4 pears, peeled, halved,
cored and cut in strips

*Caramel sauce*
1/4 cup (60 mL) water
1 cup (250 mL) sugar
2 Tbsp (30 mL) corn syrup
2/3 cup (150 mL) heavy cream (35%), hot

*For assembly*
1-1/2 cups (375 mL) heavy cream (35%)
1/4 cup (60 mL) sugar
1 tsp (5 mL) vanilla extract
12 ladyfingers, broken in four
1/4 cup (60 mL) sliced almonds,
toasted and crushed

**1 PASTRY CREAM** In a microwave oven, heat the milk and cream. Set aside.

**2** In a saucepan, combine the sugar and flour. Whisk in the egg yolks until smooth. Gradually whisk in the hot cream mixture.

**3** Bring to a boil over medium heat, whisking constantly. Remove from the heat as soon as the mixture comes to a boil. Add the vanilla.

**4** Place a sheet of plastic wrap directly on the surface of the hot pastry cream. Let cool and refrigerate until chilled, about 2 hours.

**5 CARAMELIZED PEARS** In a large skillet, heat the water and sugar until golden. Add the pears and sauté over high heat for 4 to 5 minutes. Set aside on a plate. Let cool and refrigerate until chilled.

**6 CARAMEL SAUCE** In a saucepan over high heat, bring the water, sugar and corn syrup to a boil. Cook without stirring until golden. Remove from the heat and slowly add the cream. Bring to a boil again while stirring until the mixture is smooth. Set aside in a bowl and let cool completely.

**7 ASSEMBLY** In a bowl, whip the cream, sugar and vanilla until stiff peaks form.

**8** In a 12-cup (3 L) glass serving bowl, assemble the trifle by alternating layers of half of the preparations (except for the caramel sauce, which will be divided into 4): pastry cream, ladyfingers, pears, caramel sauce and whipped cream. Repeat with the remaining ingredients, then top with whipped cream, a quarter of the caramel sauce and the crushed almonds. Use the remaining caramel sauce when serving.

**9** Refrigerate for at least 2 hours.

# BROWN SUGAR CHIFFON CAKE WITH VANILLA MANGO SALAD

*Preparation* 20 MINUTES    *Cooking* 1 HOUR    *Cooling* 3 HOURS    *Serves* 10

**Because it's made with oil instead of butter, this wonderfully spongy cake stays moist for almost a week on a covered cake stand.**

### Chiffon cake
1-1/4 cups (310 mL) unbleached all-purpose flour
1 tsp (5 mL) baking powder
1/4 tsp (1 mL) salt
6 eggs, separated
1/4 tsp (1 mL) cream of tartar
1-3/4 cups (430 mL) brown sugar
1/2 cup (125 mL) vegetable oil (canola or corn)
1/2 cup (125 mL) water
1 tsp (5 mL) vanilla extract

### Vanilla mango salad
1 vanilla bean
1/2 cup (125 mL) water
3/4 cup (180 mL) sugar
4 mangoes, peeled and cut in strips
1-1/2 cups (375 mL) heavy cream (35%)

**1 CHIFFON CAKE** With the rack in the middle position, preheat the oven to 325°F (170°C).
**2** In a bowl, combine the flour, baking powder and salt.
**3** In another bowl, beat the egg whites with the cream of tartar until soft peaks form. Gradually beat in half the brown sugar until the meringue forms stiff peaks. Set aside.
**4** In another bowl, whisk together the remaining brown sugar, egg yolks, oil, water and vanilla. Gently stir in the dry ingredients.
**5** Using a spatula, mix a quarter of the meringue into the batter. Gently fold in the remaining meringue. Pour the batter into a 10-inch (25 cm) non-stick tube cake pan (do not butter the pan). Bake until a toothpick inserted in the centre comes out clean, 55 to 60 minutes. Invert the cake pan immediately and let cool for 3 hours. Unmould.
**6 VANILLA MANGO SALAD** Using the tip of a sharp knife, split the vanilla bean lengthwise. Scrape out the seeds.
**7** In a saucepan, bring the water, 1/2 cup (125 mL) of the sugar, the vanilla pod and seeds to a boil. Add the mangoes. Remove from the heat and let cool. Drain and reserve the syrup to make a fruit salad.
**8** In a bowl, whip the cream and the remaining sugar until stiff peaks form. Refrigerate.
**9** Serve slices of cake with whipped cream and Vanilla Mango Salad.

For guys, life is a sport. The lowest golf score, the largest TV set, making the most impressive splash in the pool—it's all about being biggest and best. Same goes for cooking. A guys' meal—a real one—is like a final showdown, an athletic contest brought into the kitchen. A guys' meal is like a playoff game. Forget dainty little vegetables. A real man's meal is like a football player: meaty and distinctly lacking a light touch. And like a big game played in the pouring rain, it will mess up your uniform. There's no doubt about it: after strutting your stuff in the kitchen, you just can't wait to strut it all over town. Let's face it. When it comes to cooking, men and women are on entirely different planets. Guys are more creative, but decidedly less precise. Maybe we're a bit lazy, maybe we need some freedom. Whatever the reasons, we take stock of what we need to do, roll up our sleeves, and just do it. Sometimes there's a little spillage, a little breakage, but we're champs at recovering from setbacks. Missing an ingredient? The girls will nip out to the store. They measure everything down to the millilitre; we just eyeball it. But isn't that part of our charm?

GUYS
DON'T
READ
RECIPES

# for the big game or poker night

# ROB ROY

*Preparation* 3 MINUTES    *Makes* 1 COCKTAIL

3 Tbsp (45 mL) Scotch (1-1/2 fl oz)
4 tsp (20 mL) red vermouth
Ice cubes
1 long strip lemon zest

**1** In a cocktail shaker, combine the Scotch, vermouth and a few ice cubes.
Serve with the lemon zest in an old-fashioned glass.

# SAUSAGE ARANCINI

***Preparation*** 30 MINUTES     ***Cooking*** 45 MINUTES     ***Refrigeration*** 2 HOURS
***Makes*** 50 HORS D'OEUVRES

**You can make and fry these risotto balls in advance, refrigerate or freeze them, then reheat them before serving.**

### Risotto
1 onion, chopped
2 Tbsp (30 mL) olive oil
3/4 cup (180 mL) arborio rice
1/4 cup (60 mL) white wine
3 cups (750 mL) hot chicken broth
1/2 cup (125 mL) grated Parmigiano Reggiano
1/4 cup (60 mL) finely chopped fresh basil
1/2 lb (225 g) hot Italian sausages, casings removed (2 sausages)
Salt and pepper

### Tomato sauce
1 onion, chopped
1 clove garlic, chopped
2 Tbsp (30 mL) olive oil
19 oz (540 mL) can crushed plum tomatoes

### Breading
1/2 cup (125 mL) unbleached all-purpose flour
4 eggs, lightly beaten
2 cups (500 mL) sifted breadcrumbs

**1  RISOTTO**  In a saucepan over medium heat, soften the onion in the oil. Add the rice and cook for 1 minute, stirring to coat thoroughly with oil. Deglaze with the wine and continue cooking, stirring constantly, until almost dry.

**2**  Add the broth about 1 cup (250 mL) at a time, stirring constantly until the liquid is completely absorbed before the next addition.

**3**  The rice should be tender after about 30 minutes. Add the Parmigiano and basil and stir until the cheese melts.

**4**  Meanwhile, fry the sausage meat in a skillet, breaking the meat with a fork, until cooked through. Transfer to the risotto and stir. Adjust the seasoning.

**5**  Spread the risotto on a baking sheet and cover with plastic wrap. Refrigerate until chilled, about 2 hours.

**6  TOMATO SAUCE**  In a saucepan over medium heat, soften the onion and garlic in the oil. Season with salt and pepper. Add the tomatoes. Bring to a boil and simmer uncovered for about 15 minutes. Adjust the seasoning.

**7**  Preheat the deep fryer to 375°F (190°C). Line a baking sheet with paper towels.

**8  BREADING**  Place the flour in a shallow bowl, the eggs in a second shallow bowl and the breadcrumbs in a third.

**9**  Using a spoon, measure about 1 Tbsp (15 mL) of risotto and shape into a ball using your hands. Repeat until you have about 50 balls. Dredge in the flour, dip in egg and roll in the breadcrumbs.

**10** Sift the breadcrumbs. Dip the balls in egg and roll in breadcrumbs a second time.

**11** Fry in batches of about 8 balls, until well browned, about 2 minutes. Place on the paper towels.

**12** Place on a serving plate with a bowl of tomato sauce for dipping.

RECIPE P234

# GENERAL TAO CHICKEN WINGS

*Preparation* 30 MINUTES          *Cooking* 1 HOUR          *Serves* 4

### Chicken wings

24 chicken wings
3 Tbsp (45 mL) peanut or olive oil
Salt

### Sauce

2 tsp (10 mL) cornstarch
3 Tbsp (45 mL) soy sauce
3 Tbsp (45 mL) rice vinegar
3 Tbsp (45 mL) water
2 tsp (10 mL) toasted sesame oil
2 Tbsp (30 mL) finely chopped fresh ginger
3 cloves garlic, finely chopped
2 tsp (10 mL) sambal oelek
1/2 tsp (2.5 mL) paprika
3 Tbsp (45 mL) water
1/2 cup (125 mL) sugar
1 green onion, thinly sliced (optional)

**1 CHICKEN WINGS** With the rack in the middle position, preheat the oven to 375°F (190°C). Line a 12- x 17-inch (30 x 43 cm) baking sheet with foil.

**2** Cut the wings through the joints into 3 pieces. Discard the wing tips.

**3** Place the chicken pieces in a bowl and coat with the oil and season with salt. Arrange the wings on the baking sheet so they are not touching. Bake until the meat pulls easily from the bone, about 20 minutes per side. Broil until the skin is crisp and golden brown.

**4 SAUCE** Meanwhile, in a bowl, whisk together the cornstarch, soy sauce, rice vinegar, water, sesame oil, ginger, garlic, sambal oelek and paprika. Set aside.

**5** In a small saucepan, bring the water and sugar to a boil. Cook without stirring until the mixture turns gold. Add the soy sauce mixture. Simmer until the caramel has dissolved and the sauce is syrupy.

**6** In a large non-stick skillet over high heat, sauté the chicken in the sauce, turning the pieces until completely coated and well glazed. Garnish with green onion.

**7** To prevent the wings from becoming soft, avoid piling the wings on top of each other.

# RIBS WITH BEER BBQ SAUCE

*Preparation* 20 MINUTES  *Marinating* 8 HOURS OR LESS  *Cooking* 2 HOURS
*Serves* 4 TO 8

**Vegetables? Nah, not tonight. Most of the time, our wives make sure we get our fill.**

8 lb (3.5 kg) baby back pork ribs

*Sauce*
1 cup (250 mL) chili sauce
3/4 cup (180 mL) brown sugar
1 cup (250 mL) tomato paste
2 cups (500 mL) pale ale or white beer
6 garlic cloves, chopped
4 tsp (20 mL) Dijon mustard
4 tsp (20 mL) Worcestershire sauce
2 tsp (10 mL) ground ginger
1 tsp (5 mL) cayenne pepper (optional)
1 tsp (5 mL) salt

**1** Cut the meat between the ribs to obtain 3 ribs per piece.

**2** Place the ribs in a large saucepan and cover with lightly salted water. Bring to a boil and skim. Reduce the heat, cover and simmer gently for 45 minutes. Drain. Set aside.

**3 SAUCE** In a saucepan over medium heat, bring all the ingredients to a boil while stirring. Lower the heat and simmer for 7 or 8 minutes.

**4** In a large dish, coat the ribs with the sauce. If you have time, cover and refrigerate for several hours.

**5** With the rack in the middle position, preheat the oven to 375°F (190°C). Line 2 rimmed baking sheets with foil.

**6** Arrange the ribs on the sheets. Cover with foil and cook for 40 minutes. Remove the foil and continue cooking until the meat falls easily from the bone, about 30 minutes.

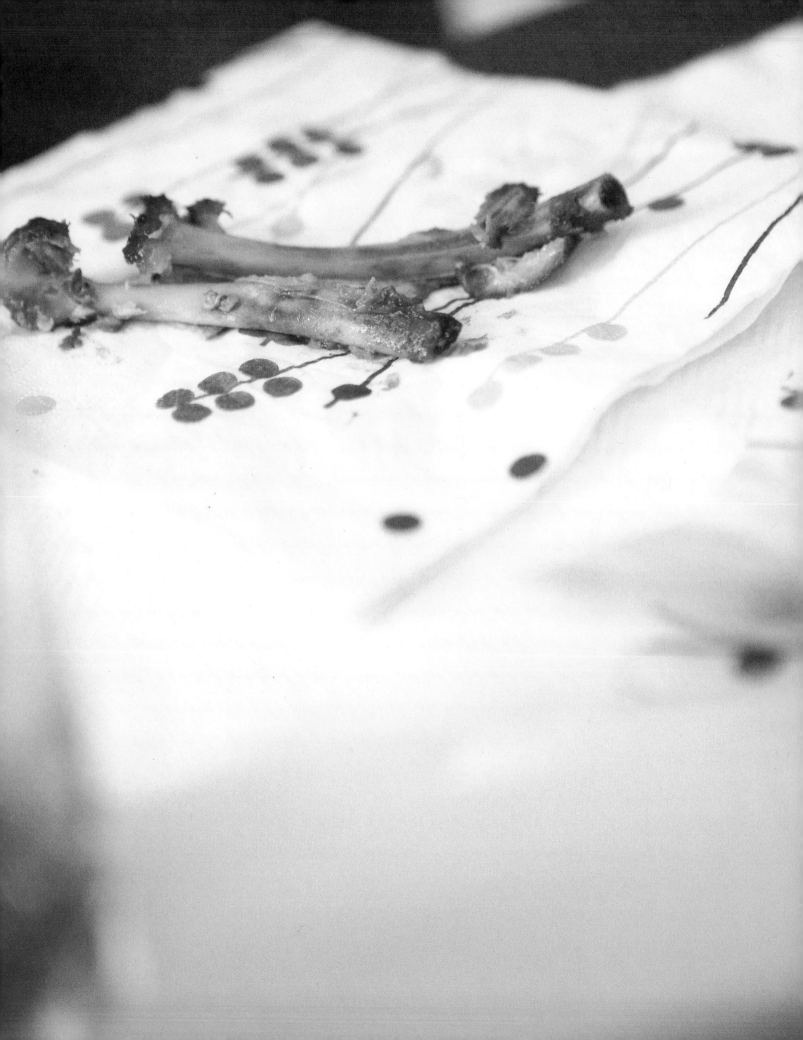

RECIPE P235

# STEAMER CLAMS WITH BEER AND CHORIZO

*Preparation* 10 MINUTES     *Cooking* 20 MINUTES     *Serves* 4 (APPETIZER)

2 cloves garlic, peeled and halved
3 Tbsp (45 mL) olive oil
1 onion, chopped
1/4 lb (115 g) chorizo, cut in rounds
2 plum tomatoes, crushed
4 sprigs fresh thyme
6 oz (170 mL) beer (1/2 bottle)
2 lb (1 kg) steamer clams or small clams, scrubbed
Salt and pepper

**1** In a saucepan over medium heat, soften the garlic in the oil. Add the onion and chorizo. Brown over medium heat. Add the tomatoes and thyme. Simmer for about 2 minutes.
**2** Add the beer and clams. Cover and bring to a boil. Stir, reduce the heat and simmer until all the clams open, about 5 minutes. Discard any unopened clams. Adjust the seasoning.

RECIPE P243

# ONION TARTE TATIN

*Preparation* 20 MINUTES  *Refrigeration* 30 MINUTES  *Cooking* 45 MINUTES
*Serves* 4 TO 6 (APPETIZER)

### Crust
1 cup (250 mL) unbleached all-purpose flour
Pinch of salt
1/4 cup (60 mL) cold unsalted butter, cubed
1 egg
1 Tbsp (15 mL) ice water (approx)

### Filling
6 cups (1.5 L) thinly sliced onions (about 5 onions)
2 Tbsp (30 mL) butter
2 Tbsp (30 mL) balsamic vinegar
3/4 cup (180 mL) grated Parmigiano Reggiano
Salt and pepper

**1 CRUST**  In a food processor, pulse the flour and salt to combine. Add the butter and pulse briefly until the butter pieces are pea-sized. Add the egg and water. Pulse until the dough just begins to hold together, adding more water if necessary. Remove the dough from the food processor and shape into a disc. Wrap in plastic and refrigerate for 30 minutes.

**2** With the rack in the middle position, preheat the oven to 400°F (200°C).

**3 FILLING**  In a 10-inch (25 cm) ovenproof non-stick skillet, sauté the onions in the butter until golden brown, about 15 minutes. Season with salt and pepper. Deglaze with the vinegar and cook for 1 more minute. Remove from the heat and let cool while you roll out the dough. Add the Parmigiano. Adjust the seasoning.

**4 ASSEMBLY**  Roll out the dough on a lightly floured surface. Cut out a circle the same size as the skillet.

**5** Lay the dough over the onions in the skillet. Bake until the crust is golden brown, about 30 minutes. Invert onto a wooden cutting board, carefully detaching any onions stuck to the bottom of the skillet. Cut into wedges. Serve with sour cream.

RECIPE P246

# VEAL MEDALLIONS WITH COFFEE–COGNAC SAUCE

*Preparation* 15 MINUTES *Cooking* 15 MINUTES *Serves* 4

1-1/2 lb (675 g) veal tenderloin medallions (4 thick slices)
1 Tbsp (15 mL) olive oil
1 shallot, finely sliced
1 clove garlic, chopped
1/4 cup (60 mL) cognac
1 cup (250 mL) chicken broth
1 recipe Butternut Squash Purée (facing page)
1/4 cup (60 mL) heavy cream (35%)
2 Tbsp (30 mL) espresso
1 Tbsp (15 mL) Dijon mustard
Salt and pepper

**1** In a skillet, brown the veal in the oil until desired doneness. Set aside on a warm plate.
**2** In the same skillet over medium heat, soften the shallot and garlic. Add the cognac and reduce by half. Add the broth, 1/4 cup (60 mL) squash purée, and the cream, coffee and mustard. Bring to a boil. Reduce until syrupy. Season with salt and pepper.
**3** Drizzle the meat with sauce and serve with Pont-Neuf Potatoes (facing page). Serve with the remaining squash purée.

# BUTTERNUT SQUASH PURÉE

*Preparation* 20 MINUTES     *Cooking* 25 MINUTES     *Serves* 4

1 onion, chopped
2 cloves garlic, chopped
3 Tbsp (45 mL) butter
6 cups (1.5 L) cubed butternut squash
1 cup (250 mL) chicken broth
Salt and pepper

**1** In a saucepan over medium heat, soften the onion and garlic in the butter. Add the squash, reduce the heat to low and cook until the squash starts to brown, about 5 minutes. Add the broth. Cover and simmer until the squash is tender, about 20 minutes.
**2** In a food processor, purée the squash until smooth. Season with salt and pepper.

# PONT-NEUF POTATOES

*Preparation* 15 MINUTES     *Cooking* 20 MINUTES     *Serves* 4

4 russet potatoes, peeled
2 cups (500 mL) duck fat (about 1 lb/500 g)
Salt

**1** Line a cookie sheet with paper towels or place a cooling rack on it.
**2** Cut the potatoes into sticks 3/4 inch (2 cm) thick.
**3** Place the potato sticks in a bowl and cover with cold water. Let stand for about 5 minutes. Drain well and pat dry with a clean tea towel.
**4** Melt the duck fat in a large skillet with high sides or in a large saucepan. Fry the potatoes in the fat over high heat, stirring gently and often, until golden brown, 15 to 20 minutes. Transfer to the cookie sheet. Season with salt.
**5** Delicious with the Veal Medallions with Coffee-Cognac Sauce (facing page) or Roasted Duck Magret with Spiced Whisky Sauce (page 168).

# BLUE CHEESE LASAGNA

*Preparation* 40 MINUTES          *Cooking* 1 HOUR 30 MINUTES          *Serves* 6

**Hey, boys! To mix things up, try goat cheese, mascarpone or any cheese with some character.**

1 recipe Béchamel (page 250)
12 lasagna noodles, cooked and coated with oil
2 cups (500 mL) grated mozzarella

*Spinach and mushroom filling*
1 lb (500 g) white mushrooms, quartered
1/4 cup (60 mL) olive oil
1/2 cup (125 mL) white wine
3 shallots, chopped
Two 6 oz (170 g) bags spinach, chopped
Salt and pepper

*Cheese filling*
1 onion, chopped
1 Tbsp (15 mL) butter
5 oz (150 g) blue cheese, cubed
1 lb (475 g) container ricotta
1/2 cup (125 mL) fresh basil
1 egg

**1 MUSHROOM AND SPINACH FILLING** In a large skillet over high heat, brown the mushrooms in 2 Tbsp (30 mL) oil. Season with salt and pepper. Add the wine and reduce until dry. Set aside in a large bowl.

**2** In the same skillet over medium heat, soften the shallots in the remaining oil. Add the spinach and cook until the water is completely evaporated. Mix the spinach and mushrooms and add 1/2 cup (125 mL) béchamel. Adjust the seasoning. Set aside.

**3 CHEESE FILLING** In a skillet over medium heat, soften the onion in the butter. Set aside in a bowl and let cool.

**4** In a food processor, purée the onions, blue cheese, ricotta, basil and egg. Season with salt and pepper. Set aside.

**5** With the rack in the middle position, preheat the oven to 375°F (190°C).

**6 ASSEMBLY** Spread a third of the béchamel in an 8- x 14-inch (20 x 35 cm) baking dish. Cover with a layer of noodles. Cover with the spinach and mushroom filling. Cover with another layer of noodles. Cover with the cheese filling. Cover with another layer of noodles. Cover with a third of the béchamel. Add a final layer of noodles. Top with the remaining béchamel and sprinkle with the mozzarella.

**7** Bake for 40 to 45 minutes, then brown under the broiler.

# BÉCHAMEL

*Preparation* 5 MINUTES      *Cooking* 15 MINUTES      *Makes* 3 CUPS (750 ML)

1/4 cup (60 mL) butter
1/4 cup (60 mL) unbleached all-purpose flour
3 cups (750 mL) milk
Pinch nutmeg
Salt and pepper

**1** Melt the butter in a saucepan over medium heat. Add the flour and cook for 1 minute while stirring. Whisk in the milk. Stir until the mixture boils. Add the nutmeg. Season with salt and pepper. Reduce the heat and simmer gently for 5 minutes, stirring frequently to prevent the sauce from sticking to the bottom of the saucepan.

# RIB ROAST
# WITH BÉARNAISE SAUCE

*Preparation* 30 MINUTES     *Cooking* 1 HOUR 30 MINUTES     *Resting* 15 MINUTES     *Serves* 6

### Roast
One 4-1/2 lb (2 kg) rib roast, deboned and tied back on the bone
1 Tbsp (15 mL) whole-grain mustard
1 Tbsp (15 mL) Dijon mustard
1 Tbsp (15 mL) melted butter
2 tsp (10 mL) brown sugar
2 Tbsp (30 mL) olive oil
12 medium carrots
3 leeks, white part only, cut in 4-inch (10 cm) lengths
3 onions, cut in 1/4-inch (0.5 cm) slices
3/4 cup (180 mL) chicken broth
Salt and pepper

### Béarnaise sauce
1/3 cup (75 mL) white wine vinegar
1/2 shallot, chopped
1/4 tsp (1 mL) cracked black pepper
2 egg yolks
1-1/4 cups (310 mL) melted butter, at room temperature
1 Tbsp (15 mL) chopped fresh tarragon

**1 ROAST** With the rack in the middle position, preheat the oven to 375°F (190°C).

**2** Season the meat on all sides with salt and pepper and place in a roasting pan bone-side down.

**3** In a bowl, mix the mustards, butter and brown sugar. Brush the mixture on the meat. Insert a meat thermometer in the centre of the roast. Roast for 20 minutes.

**4** Coat the carrots, leeks and onions with oil. Season with salt and pepper. Scatter the vegetables around the roast and add the broth. Continue roasting until the thermometer reads 129°F (54°C) for rare, or 145°F (63°C) for medium, about 1 hour and 10 minutes. Set the roast on a plate, tent with foil and let stand for about 15 minutes.

**5 BÉARNAISE SAUCE** In a saucepan, bring the vinegar, shallot and pepper to a boil. Reduce until 2 Tbsp (30 mL) of liquid remain.

**6** In the top part of a double boiler set over simmering water, whisk the egg yolks and the vinegar reduction until thick and frothy. Off the heat, add the butter in a thin stream, whisking constantly. Add the tarragon.

**7** Untie and carve the roast. Serve with the vegetables, Béarnaise sauce and some nice mashed potatoes.

RECIPE P256

RECIPE P257

# CARAMEL NUT PIE

*Preparation* 15 MINUTES  *Cooking* 35 MINUTES  *Refrigeration* 1 HOUR 30 MINUTES
*Serves* 8 TO 10

### Shortbread crust
1-1/4 cups (310 mL) unbleached all-purpose flour
1/4 cup (60 mL) sugar
1/2 tsp (2.5 mL) baking powder
1/4 tsp (1 mL) salt
1/4 cup (60 mL) cold unsalted butter, cubed
1 egg, lightly beaten
2 Tbsp (30 mL) cold water (approx)

### Filling
1/4 cup (60 mL) water
1-1/2 cups (375 mL) sugar
1 cup (250 mL) heavy cream (35%), hot
2 Tbsp (30 mL) semi-salted butter
2-1/4 cups (560 mL) toasted mixed nuts (blanched almonds and hazelnuts, pecans, macadamia nuts, cashews, etc.)

**1** With the rack in the middle position, preheat the oven to 350°F (180°C).
**2 SHORTBREAD CRUST** In a food processor, combine the flour, sugar, baking powder and salt. Add the butter and process until the mixture resembles coarse sand. Add the egg and water. Mix until the dough just starts to hold together. Remove the dough from the processor. Using your fingertips, press the dough into a tart pan with a removable bottom, 9 inches (23 cm) across and 1-1/4 inches (3 cm) deep. Bake until the crust is golden brown, about 25 minutes. Let cool.
**3 FILLING** In a saucepan, bring the water and sugar to a boil. Simmer without stirring until the mixture turns golden. Remove from the heat and slowly add the cream, taking care to avoid spattering. Bring to a boil, stirring until fully mixed. Fold in the butter and nuts. Let cool for 30 minutes. Pour into the crust and refrigerate until chilled.

# ESPRESSO BROWNIES

*Preparation* 20 MINUTES    *Cooking* 30 MINUTES    *Refrigeration* 4 HOURS    *Serves* 6

3/4 cup (180 mL) unbleached all-purpose flour, sifted
1/4 cup (60 mL) cocoa powder, sifted
1/4 tsp (1 mL) salt
6 oz (170 g) semi-sweet chocolate, chopped
3/4 cup (180 mL) cold unsalted butter, cubed
1 cup (250 mL) sugar
3 eggs
6 small scoops vanilla ice cream
3/4 cup (180 mL) hot espresso

**1** With the rack in the middle position, preheat the oven to 325°F (170°C). Line the bottom of an 8-inch (20 cm) square baking pan with parchment paper, letting the paper overhang 2 sides, and butter the other 2 sides.
**2** In a bowl, combine the flour, cocoa powder and salt. Set aside.
**3** In the top part of a double boiler, melt the chocolate and the butter. Remove the top part of the boiler. Whisk in the sugar. Add the eggs one at a time and whisk for 2 minutes. Gently stir in the dry ingredients using a wooden spoon. Pour the batter into the pan. Bake until the centre is set but still moist, 25 to 30 minutes.
**4** Let cool in the pan, about 4 hours. Unmould and cut into small squares.
**5** Place brownie pieces in coffee cups. Top with scoops of ice cream and drizzle with a small amount of espresso.

# RUSTIC APPLE, PEAR AND DATE TART

***Preparation*** 25 MINUTES          ***Refrigeration*** 30 MINUTES          ***Cooking*** 50 MINUTES          ***Serves*** 8

### Pastry
2 cups (500 mL) unbleached all-purpose flour
2 Tbsp (30 mL) sugar
Pinch salt
3/4 cup (180 mL) cold unsalted butter, cubed
1 egg
1/4 cup (60 mL) ice water (approx)

### Filling
6 apples, peeled, cored and sliced
6 pears, peeled, cored and sliced
1 cup (250 mL) Medjool dates, halved and pitted
1/2 cup (125 mL) sugar or brown sugar

**1 PASTRY** In a food processor, pulse the flour, sugar and salt to combine. Add the butter and pulse until the butter pieces are pea-sized. Add the egg and water. Pulse until the dough just begins to hold together, adding more water if necessary. Remove the dough and shape into a disc. Cover and refrigerate for 30 minutes.

**2** With the rack in the bottom position, preheat the oven to 375°F (190°C). Invert a 12- x 17-inch (30 x 43 cm) baking sheet and line the bottom with parchment paper.

**3** On a floured surface, roll the dough into a rectangle slightly larger than the baking sheet. Place the dough on the inverted sheet. Refrigerate for 30 minutes.

**4 FILLING** In a bowl, gently toss the fruit with the sugar. Arrange the fruit in the middle of the dough, leaving a margin of about 3 inches (8 cm) on all sides. Fold the edges of the dough inward to make a tart measuring about 9 x 14 inches (23 x 36 cm).

**5** Bake until the crust is golden, 45 to 50 minutes. Let cool.

**6** Slide the tart onto a large cutting board. Cut into squares and serve from the board.

**7** Serve with caramel sauce (page 218), crème fraîche or vanilla ice cream.

# index
## BY CATEGORIES

## Sauces

BÉARNAISE SAUCE  P251
BÉCHAMEL SAUCE  P250
BEER BBQ SAUCE  P235
CARAMEL SAUCE  P218
CHOCOLATE SAUCE  P213
COFFEE CARAMEL SAUCE  P122
COFFEE-COGNAC SAUCE  P246
HERBES SALÉES SALSA VERDE  P101
MAPLE-BEET SAUCE  P138
PUTTANESCA SAUCE  P062
SPICED WHISKY SAUCE  P168
SUN-DRIED TOMATO AND PUMPKIN SEED PESTO  P070
TARTAR SAUCE  P074, P114
TOMATO SAUCE  P077, P230
WATERCRESS SAUCE  P167

## Pastry

CHOUX PASTRY  P213
PIE CRUST  P258
SHORTBREAD PIE CRUST  P256

## Main courses

4-HOUR MILK-BRAISED PORK  P209
5-MINUTE COCONUT-MILK FISH  P062
AMERICAN-STYLE DOUBLE CHEESEBURGERS  P110
ATLANTIC TOMCOD MEUNIÈRE  P130
BLUE CHEESE LASAGNA  P249
CABBAGE STUFFED WITH THREE CHEESES  P201
CHICKEN LEGS WITH HONEY AND ROSEMARY  P060
CHICKEN WITH MORELS  P204
COD WITH SUN-DRIED TOMATO AND PUMPKIN SEED PESTO  P073
CREAM-FREE PENNE ROMANOFF  P066
CRISPY SHREDDED WHEAT™ FISH FILLETS  P074
GENERAL TAO CHICKEN WINGS  P234
GRILLED HALIBUT WITH HERBES SALÉES SALSA VERDE  P101
LAMB SHANKS GLAZED WITH BUCKWHEAT HONEY  P210
LEMON AND GARLIC SHRIMP KEBABS  P063
MACARONI AND CHEESE  P075
MINI PO' BOY SANDWICHES  P114
PASTA WITH PUTTANESCA SAUCE  P062
PEROGIES  P205
PORK TENDERLOINS GLAZED WITH MAPLE-BEET SAUCE  P138
PORK TENDERLOINS WITH BACON BREADING  P078
PORTUGUESE COD CASSEROLE  P212
RIB ROAST WITH BÉARNAISE SAUCE  P251
RIBS WITH BEER BBQ SAUCE  P235
RISOTTO À LA WHATEVER  P064
ROAST CHICKEN WITH FOIE GRAS  P173
ROASTED DUCK MAGRET WITH SPICED WHISKY SAUCE  P168
SKATE WITH WATERCRESS SAUCE  P167
SLOW-COOKED BEEF WITH RED WINE  P137
SPINACH POLPETTI WITH TOMATO SAUCE  P077
VEAL MEDALLIONS WITH COFFEE-COGNAC SAUCE  P246

# index
## BY CATEGORIES

with lime +++ Dukka +++ Foie gras au torchon +++ Leeks and celery vinaigrette +++
Onion Tarte Tatin +++ Oysters with pink grapefruit +++ Red bell pepper spread +++ Sausage
arancini +++ Scallop tartare +++ Smoked trout rillettes +++ Steamer clams with beer and
chorizo +++ Beef "cappuccino" with parsnip foam +++ Cabbage and beet soup +++ Choisy
soup +++ Cream of brie soup +++ Cream of shallot soup +++ Fish and seafood chowder
+++ Fish stracciatella with herbs +++ Minestrone +++ Onion soup with beer +++ Asparagus
Caesar salad +++ Bacon-mustard butter +++ Brown tarragon butter +++ Buttered sugar snap
peas +++ Butternut squash purée +++ Cauliflower purée +++ Celery roasted with 20 cloves
garlic +++ Classic mashed potatoes +++ Herbes salées +++ Leeks and celery vinaigrette +++
Lemon-lime butter +++ Mashed sweet potatoes +++ Miniature vegetables roasted in olive oil
+++ Montreal steak spice +++ Mushroom duxelles +++ Pont-Neuf potatoes +++ Scalloped
Jerusalem artichokes +++ Vanilla-pink peppercorn potato purée +++ Béarnaise sauce +++
Béchamel sauce +++ Caramel sauce +++ Chocolate sauce +++ Herbes salées salsa verde +++
Puttanesca sauce +++ Spiced whisky sauce +++ Sun-dried tomato and pumpkin seed pesto
+++ Tartar sauce +++ Tomato sauce +++ Watercress sauce +++ Choux pastry +++ Pie crust
+++ Shortbread pie crust +++ 4-hour milk-braised pork +++ 5-minute coconut-milk fish +++ American-style double cheeseburgers +++ Atlantic tomcod meunière +++ Blue cheese lasagna +++
Cabbage stuffed with three cheeses +++ Chicken legs with honey and rosemary +++ Chicken
with morels +++ Cod with sun-dried tomato and pumpkin seed pesto +++ Cream-free penne
Stroganoff +++ Crispy Shredded Wheat™ fish fillets +++ General Tao chicken wings +++ Grilled
halibut with herbes salées salsa verde +++ Lamb shanks glazed with buckwheat honey +++
Lemon and garlic shrimp kebabs +++ Macaroni and cheese +++ Mini po' boy sandwiches +++
Pasta with puttanesca sauce +++ Perogies +++ Pork tenderloins glazed with maple-beer
sauce +++ Pork tenderloins with bacon breading +++ Portuguese cod casserole +++ Rib roast
with Béarnaise sauce +++ Ribs with beer BBQ sauce +++ Risotto à la whatever +++ Roast chicken with foie gras +++ Roasted duck magret with spiced whisky sauce +++ Skate with watercress sauce +++ Slow-cooked beef with red wine +++ Spinach polpetti with tomato sauce +++
Veal medallions with coffee-cognac sauce +++ Apple and maple verrine +++ Banana split
with cranberry compote and coffee caramel sauce +++ Beet cakes with mascarpone cream +++
Blueberry pudding on the barbecue +++ Brown sugar chiffon cake with vanilla mango
salad +++ Caramel nut pie +++ Chocolate carrot cake +++ Chocolate pudding +++ Espresso
brownies +++ Flambéed morello cherries +++ Honey-roasted figs with almond praline ice
cream +++ Iced maple-pecan praline parfait +++ Maple-pecan biscotti +++ Mascarpone-Tiramisù +++ Mini Tarte Tatin +++ Muscat and red grape cake +++ Perfect vanilla cake +++ Portuguese flan +++ Profiteroles +++ Quick raspberry mousse +++ Rustic apple and summer
berry tart +++ Rustic apple, pear and date tart +++ Strawberry and balsamic vinegar sundaes +++ Trifle with pears and caramel +++ Vanilla icing +++ White chocolate pots de crème
with passionfruit jelly +++ Breakfast club sandwiches +++ Buckwheat crêpe burritos +++
Cheddar and onion baguettes +++ Cranberry scones +++ Fiddlehead omelette +++ Granola
+++ Honey-orange butter +++ Orange and grapefruit salad with a twist +++ Peanut butter
banana muffins with strawberry jam +++ Quick strawberry-maple syrup jam +++ Quilt pie
with asparagus, eggs and ham +++ Sundae brunch +++ Lichee martini +++ Mango and strawberry smoothies +++ Rob Roy +++ Crab and strawberry salad with lime +++ Dukka +++ Foie
gras au torchon +++ Leeks and celery vinaigrette +++ Onion tarte Tatin +++ Oysters with pink
grapefruit +++ Red bell pepper spread +++ Sausage arancini +++ Scallop tartare +++ Smoked
trout rillettes +++ Steamer clams with beer and chorizo +++ Beef "cappuccino" with parsnip
foam +++ Cabbage and beet soup +++ Choisy soup +++ Cream of brie soup +++ Cream of
shallot soup +++ Fish and seafood chowder +++ Fish stracciatella with herbs +++ Minestrone
+++ Onion soup with beer +++ Asparagus Caesar salad +++ Bacon-mustard butter +++ Brown
tarragon butter +++ Buttered sugar snap peas +++ Butternut squash purée +++ Cauliflower

# index
## BY INGREDIENTS

# index
## BY INGREDIENTS

## Pasta

## Pork

## Potatoes

## Salads

## Sandwiches

## Sausages

## Seafood

# index
## BY INGREDIENTS

...uese flan +++ Trifle with pears and caramel +++ Blue cheese lasagna +++ Buckwheat ...burritos +++ Cabbage stuffed with three cheeses +++ Cheddar and onion baguettes ++ ...eam of brie soup +++ Cream-free penne Romanoff +++ Fiddlehead omelette +++ Macar ...d cheese +++ Mascarpone-free tiramisù +++ Onion soup with beer +++ Onion Tarte Tati... ...Perogies +++ Risotto à la whatever +++ Spinach polpetti with tomato sauce +++ Chick... ...s with honey and rosemary +++ Chicken with morels +++ General Tao chicken wings ++... ...ast chicken with foie gras +++ Chocolate carrot cake +++ Chocolate pudding +++ Espr... ...brownies +++ Profiteroles +++ White chocolate pots de crème with passionfruit jelly ++... ...inute coconut-milk fish +++ Banana splits with cranberry compote and coffee carame... ...ce +++ Espresso brownies +++ Veal medallions with coffee-cognac sauce +++ Banana ...its with cranberry compote and coffee caramel sauce +++ Cranberry scones +++ Gran... ...Scallop tartare +++ Foie gras au torchon +++ Roast chicken with foie gras +++ Roaste... ...k magret with spiced whisky sauce +++ Breakfast club sandwiches +++ Fiddlehead ...elette +++ Fish stracciatella with herbs +++ Quilt pie with asparagus, eggs and ham +... ...inute coconut-milk fish +++ Atlantic tomcod meunière +++ Cod with sun-dried tomato ...d pumpkin seed pesto +++ Crispy Shredded Wheat™ fish fillets +++ Fish and seafood ...owder +++ Fish stracciatella with herbs +++ Grilled halibut with herbes salées salsa ve... ...Portuguese cod casserole +++ Skate with watercress sauce +++ Smoked trout rillettes ...ple and maple verrine +++ Banana splits with cranberry compote and coffee caramel ...ce +++ Blueberry pudding on the barbecue +++ Sundae brunch +++ Flambéed morello ...rries +++ Honey-roasted figs with almond praline ice cream +++ Mango and strawber... ...oothies +++ Mini Tarte Tatin +++ Orange and grapefruit salad with a twist +++ Quick r... ...ry mousse +++ Quick strawberry-maple syrup jam +++ Rustic apple and summer berr... ...t +++ Rustic apple, pear and date tart +++ Strawberry and balsamic vinegar sundaes +... ...le with pears and caramel +++ Vanilla mango salad +++ Quilt pie with asparagus, eg... ...d ham +++ Lamb shanks glazed with buckwheat honey +++ Apple and maple verrine ...d maple-pecan praline parfait +++ Maple-pecan biscotti +++ Pork tenderloins glazed ...h maple-beet sauce +++ Quick strawberry-maple syrup jam +++ Blue cheese lasagna ...Cream-free penne Romanoff +++ Macaroni and cheese +++ Pasta with puttanesca sau... ...+++ Perogies +++ Spinach polpetti with tomato sauce +++ 4-hour milk-braised pork +++... ...k tenderloins glazed with maple-beet sauce +++ Pork tenderloins with bacon breadin... ...Ribs with beer BBQ sauce +++ Cabbage and beet soup +++ Cabbage stuffed with thre... ...eeses +++ Choisy soup +++ Classic mashed potatoes +++ Fish and seafood chowder +++ ...ogies +++ Pont-Neuf potatoes +++ Portuguese cod casserole +++ Vanilla-pink pepper-... ...n potato purée +++ Crab and strawberry salad with lime +++ Orange and grapefruit s... ...l with a twist +++ Vanilla mango salad +++ Breakfast club sandwiches +++ Cheddar an... ...on baguettes +++ Mini po' boy sandwiches +++ Buckwheat crêpe burritos +++ Sausage ...ancini +++ Steamer clams with beer and chorizo +++ Crab and strawberry salad with l... ...Fish and seafood chowder +++ Lemon and garlic shrimp kebabs +++ Mini po' boy san... ...ches +++ Oysters with pink grapefruit +++ Risotto à la whatever +++ Scallop tartare +++ ...amer clams with beer and chorizo +++ Crab and strawberry salad with lime +++ Mang... ...d strawberry smoothies +++ Quick strawberry-maple syrup jam +++ Rustic apple and ...mmer berry tart +++ Strawberry and balsamic vinegar sundaes +++ Cream-free penne ...noff +++ Minestrone +++ Pasta with puttanesca sauce +++ Sausage arancini +++ Spina ...lpetti with tomato sauce +++ Sun-dried tomato and pumpkin seed pesto +++ Tomato so... ...+++ Veal medallions with coffee-cognac sauce +++ Asparagus Caesar salad +++ Butte... ...gar snap peas +++ Butternut squash purée +++ Cauliflower purée +++ Celery roasted w... ...ves of garlic +++ Classic mashed potatoes +++ Leeks and celery vinaigrette +++ Mashe... ...eet potatoes +++ Miniature vegetables roasted in olive oil +++ Mushroom duxelles +++ ...t-Neuf potatoes +++ Scalloped Jerusalem artichokes +++ Vanilla-pink peppercorn po...

NATALY Brigitte PIERRETTE SONIA Kareen

JULES

CAROLINE MARYSE Christian CAROLINE B.

Carole ANNE

SYLVAIN BENOIT GINETTE françois-nicolas

MARTIN Christine

maTT ISABELLE

the taste-testers ETIENNE